# Guelph

## Versifiers

OF THE

## 19th Century

\*\*\*

COMPILED, EDITED, INTRODUCTION AND APPENDICES BY
### DAVID J. KNIGHT
(BA, MA, MPHIL)

---

FOREWORD BY
SUSAN RATCLIFFE

"The weather is Prognosticatory"
Guelph *Mercury* - 7 January, 1876

\*\*\*

GUELPH:
VOCAMUS EDITIONS
2014

PUBLISHED BY VOCAMUS EDITIONS

BOOK DESIGN AND LAYOUT BY DAVID J. KNIGHT AND JEREMY LUKE HILL

COVER POSTCARD IMAGE OF THE SPEED RIVER BY MOONLIGHT
COURTESY OF GUELPH MUSEUMS (ARCHIVE #1986.18.268)

MARBLED PAPERS BY MONIKA HAUCK

CALLIGRAPHY BY DANIEL J. KNIGHT

ORIGINAL 19TH CENTURY IMAGES ON PAGES IV AND 180 FROM HETTY HAZELWOOD (1871)
AND ON PAGE 145, FROM THE GUELPH DAILY MERCURY (1879).

Vocamus Press:
130 Dublin Street, North
Guelph, Ontario, Canada
N1H 4N4

www.vocamus.net

*First Edition* 2014

ISBN 13: 978-1-928171-05-8 (PBK)
ISBN 13: 978-1-928171-06-5 (EBK)

# Acknowledgements

I would like to thank my parents and the generosity of friends who have made this book possible, especially Sona Mincoff, Andrew Vowles, Tanya Korigan, and the proofreaders: Nick Ford (Southampton, UK), Jeremy Luke Hill (Guelph), and Scott McGovern (Guelph).

I would also like to acknowledge the following:

Susan Ratcliffe for writing the Foreword

Monika Hauck for original marbled paper designs

Zilla Oddy (Archive and Local History Assistant; Heritage Hub, Hawick, Scotland)

The descendants of John Inglis, namely Rita and Alan Storie of Hawick, Scotland

The Guelph Public Library Archives, namely Darcy Hiltz.

University of Guelph Archival and Special Collections (McLaughlin Library), namely Melissa McAfee, for professionally identifying the rarity of John Inglis' poetry volume.

Scott McGovern for his tactful, tactical encouragement

John Parkyn (member of the Guelph Historical Society) for his enthusiasm

Jeremy Luke Hill of Vocamus Press and Vocamus Editions

Nick Ford for translating French and German phrases by "Diogenes Redivivus"

Shannon Christie for clarifying details of the Petrie genealogy

James Gordon for lending me his CD: *Song of Our City*

Ed Butts, for his interest and encouragement

*and*

Daniel J. Knight for the calligraphic rendering of the title word "Guelph"

\* \* \*

# Contents

\*\*\*

# Foreword

As Canadians, we sometimes feel that only those who write or are celebrated or buried in foreign places are worthy of renown or recognition. Consider the words of Thomas Hardy when he was told that novels are worthwhile only if they cover large extents of country: "the domestic emotions have throbbed in Wessex nooks with as much intensity as in the palaces of Europe and that anyhow there was quite enough human nature in Wessex for one man's literary purpose...the people are...beings in whose hearts and minds that which is apparently local should be really universal."[1]

In this new compilation of thirty-two poets who wrote in nineteenth-century Guelph, David J. Knight has demonstrated that our locally-grown writers express their domestic emotions just as throbbingly as the best of the poets of the wider Western world.

In this collection, Knight shows that our own city of Guelph was indeed a fertile breeding ground for poets over its first hundred years. He includes poems by city founders and engineers, by early settlers and farmers, by newspaper editors and hotel keepers. Several poets come to us known only by their initials and their writing, leaving us to speculate on their identity and background.

Through Knight's extensive research into local sources, we can read the "domestic emotions" of early Guelph writers as they express their loves, their losses, their despair, their joy in the nature surrounding them, their political beliefs and sometimes their deep yearning for the lands they left behind.

All of us who love Guelph's heritage will also appreciate Knight's interesting account of Guelph newspapers, bookstores, libraries, printers and book binders. His list of all books published in Guelph in its first seventy-five years shows that our city was fostering all types of writing, not just poetry.

*Guelph Versifiers* is a fine addition to our knowledge of Guelph and will increase our appreciation of its artistic and literary legacy.

SUSAN RATCLIFFE
July 2014
Guelph

---

[1] "General Preface" to the 1912 edition of Thomas Hardy's Wessex novels.

# Introduction

What is unique about Guelph? What makes it unlike any other place in the world? A multitude of communities have music, theatre and film festivals. Craftspeople, artisans, artists, breweries and activists also exist in numerous other places. The answer is that Guelph was founded by a writer of fiction. A versifier. An author of prose and poetry. John Galt's Guelph is perhaps globally unique in this respect. There appear to be only two other close contenders, Tokyo and Sabbioneta. Edo (later Tokyo) was already a small fishing village when Ōta Dōkan, a Samurai-warrior poet, founded Edo Castle in 1457. Sabbioneta, in Lombardy, Italy, was founded by Vespasiano Gonzaga Colonna from 1556 to 1591. However, while he wrote descriptions of engineering works, it is dubious whether he wrote verse.

John Galt, primarily remembered internationally as a Scottish novelist, found himself in the unique position with the Canada Company to settle the Huron Tract. Accordingly, his foundation of Guelph in 1827 can be viewed as a truly exceptional case of a word-smith creating a real location, influenced, to varying degrees, by his fictive imagination. The foundation of Goderich, also in 1827, on the shore of Lake Huron, by Galt's colleague William "Tiger" Dunlop does not share this conceptual stratigraphy, as Dunlop, while the author of informative memoirs, was no versifier.[2]

In identifying Guelph's uniqueness, it is not surprising that a specific term does not exist for a city founded by a writer of fiction - perhaps "Graphopolis" would do. Interestingly, Guelph was mentioned satirically in the 1833 *Fraser's Magazine for Town and Country* (Volume 7, page 436) as "Galtopolis." By studying the versifiers of Guelph, perhaps it may be possible to identify "Galtopolitan," "Guelpolitan," "Guelphic," or "Guelvan" characteristics in the material reality of the imagined city.

This unique aspect of Guelph has a number of intriguing repercussions worth exploring in regard to its intangible heritage of fictive creation. The Guelph versifiers unearthed and remembered in this collection cover the 19th century (1827-1899). The term "versifier" is used here to distinguish those who write verse, usually in poetic form, from writers of prose.

What were the poetic muses of Guelph that inspired residents and visitors to compose verse? The answer lies, to a large extent, in the three arteries at the heart of Guelph, together creating the soul of the city. The first is the historical detail and context of its foundation by John Galt on St. George's Day, 23 April, 1827. The second is the conceptual meaning of its situation and relation to the lineage of 15th century Renaissance humanist concepts of the ideal city. The third is the physical topography of Guelph at the

---

[2] Neither was Guelph's ex-postmaster Silas R. Dale, who travelled south and founded a community in North Dakota on 8 March, 1887 - naming it Guelph after his hometown.

confluence of two rivers, the Speed and Eramosa, and the original street-plan that responds to and augments these locational attributes. These arteries set the stage for social expansion via technological advancements, complimented by entrepreneurial experimentation and the integration of a reading/writing public engaged with local newspapers, publishers, libraries, hotel reading rooms and bookstores. For instance, the St. Andrew's Society of Guelph had a "Bard of Guelph," and by 1890 there had blossomed an Ontario Agricultural College Literary Society and a Paisley Block Literary Society. A short notice in the Guelph *Weekly Herald* (29 January, 1891) announced the following:

> A literary society is being organized in connection with the Collegiate Institute.[3] A meeting was held on Tuesday afternoon to nominate officers, &c., which was presided over by Principal Tytler.[4] The society starts under favourable auspices.

These various aspects of Guelph's heart intertwine to provide a versifier's muse, in tandem with the flora and fauna of the Speed and Eramosa rivers; the now-lost forested wilderness, the glacial drumlins and eskers, limestone, underground streams and springs, valleys, wetlands and surrounding agricultural lands. The older native memories embedded in the transhumance fishing and hunting routes along the ancient valleys may also have acted as primeval echoes heard occasionally by sensitive, versifying European emigres.

The original street-plan of Guelph, laid out and executed under the direction of John Galt, Charles Prior and Samuel Strickland, has consistently been described as resembling a contemporary 1827 "Lady's fan." This over-simplistic descriptive summary requires reassessment in light of the conceptual influence of the ideal European city. The plaque below a 1979 bronze bust of John Galt by John Miecznikowski outside the old Guelph city hall states that Galt's "travels included Buffalo, New York and Detroit, Michigan which used a radial baroque design connected with a larger grid of streets... also influenced by the New Town movement used in Edinburgh, Scotland which emphasized vistas, wide streets, public squares and dramatic views of public buildings."[5] Not to mention Galt's more relevant extensive travels throughout Europe, the Mediterranean basin and the Levant, where he encountered cities that had been founded during the Roman empire and earlier.

The importance of the initial urban layout of Guelph is that it is the original versification of the chosen landscape. It inscribes upon a selected prominent level, and dramatically rising drumlin, aspirations of future civic and industrial development while at the same time grounded in memories of Scotland, England and Ireland. Hence, the historic core of Guelph boasts street names such as Glasgow, Edinburgh, Paisley, London,

---

[3] Later, the Guelph Collegiate Vocational Institute (G.C.V.I.).

[4] St. Patrick's School in Guelph, built in 1878, was later renamed in honor of educator William Tytler. Tytler School was closed in June, 2013.

[5] The plaque does not name the author of this summation.

Oxford, Cambridge, Woolwich, Surrey, Norfolk, Sussex, Essex, Dublin and Cork. The wide Macdonell[6] and Wyndham[7] streets have pretensions of grandeur, harkening to the processional boulevards of older European cities. The founding act of felling a large maple tree became the pivot from which major streets emanated. St. George's Square is an immense public piazza that has spent most of its life as a public transportation hub. The original Market Square was an immense open area bounded by the city hall and hotels.

Guelph also possesses a number of streets named after famous versifiers, including Byron Court (Lord Byron), Chesterfield Avenue (Philip Stanhope, 4th Earl of Chesterfield), Chesterton Lane (G.K. Chesterton), Devere Drive (Aubrey DeVere), Eliot Place (Thomas Stearns Eliot), Galt Avenue (John Galt), Joyce Place (James Joyce), Kingsley Court (Charles Kingsley), Leacock Avenue (Stephen Butler Leacock), Lindsay Court (Nicholas Vachel Lindsay), Longfellow (Henry Wadsworth Longfellow), Shakespeare Drive, Sheridan (Richard Brimley Sheridan), and Yeats Court (William Butler Yeats).[8] Further, Flanders Road and Waverley Drive were named, respectively, after McCrae's famous poem "In Flanders Fields," and Sir Walter Scott's influential *Waverley* novels.

When navigating the conceptual cartography of Guelph, one cannot overlook the atemporal, fictive and coincidental. For instance, Ayn Rand's *Atlas Shrugged* (1957) has the main character, one John Galt (apparently not named after the Scottish novelist), founding an ideal city in the wilderness which he names Gulch. Gulch and Guelph are not separated by any great gulf in terms of their fictional/factual quality. If Gulch holds a reality through its literary expression, perhaps we can consider Guelph as a reflection of this - as a fiction; a versified extension of Galt's pen wherein real people dwell and versify.

In 1937, Guelph held a Book Fair with works by local authors, some of whom date to the 19th century and are included in this collection. The main organizer was Florence Partridge, "who was complimented by the representatives of the Association of Canadian Bookmen present." Also acknowledged was Alice Cabeldu, who "arranged the display of books by Guelph authors, and books written about Guelph." The article covering this exhibition[9] appeared in the Guelph *Mercury* on 29 October, 1937, and has a section on local Guelph writers that is worth fully citing here:

> It was almost impossible to push one's way into the corner containing the
> Guelph exhibit, where there was much of rather amazing interest. Writers con-

[6] Named after Bishop Alexander MacDonnell, the first Roman Catholic Bishop of Upper Canada (Irwin 1998:44). The spelling of the Guelph street has wavered throughout it's history - usually now Macdonell.

[7] Named after George Francis Wyndham, 4th Earl of Egremont (1786-1845). G.F. Wyndham was an English nobleman, receiving his first Royal Navy commission in 1799 and attaining the rank of Captain in 1812, commanding "the Bristol troop-ship in the Mediterranean, and at the siege of Tarragona" (*The Gentleman's Magazine*, 1845; Volume 178, page 539).

[8] Refer to Irwin 1998:30,31,34,35,37,41,42,43,51,58.

[9] One week later (5 November, 1937), a complimentary review of this Guelph Book Fair appeared in *The Globe & Mail*.

tributing to this exhibit included Lt.-Col. John McCrae, Anne Sutherland,[10] George A. Drew,[11] O. J. Stevenson,[12] John D. Higinbotham,[13] Elinor Glyn,[14] David Allan,[15] A. E. Byerly,[16] M. T. Scroggie,[17] Rupert Broadfoot,[18] Maryan Beattie,[19] John Galt, James Gay, John McLean; Mary Leslie, the first Canadian woman author, who wrote under the pen name of James Thomas Jones;[20] H. W. Peterson, the first German publisher in Canada, whose book on display was published in 1839 and is in German; Frank Coffee; Norman Guthrie who wrote under the pen name of John Crichton;[21] educational books by H. H. Dead, George Day and J. E. Durrant, music books by Laura Lemon,[22] Elizabeth Fletcher, Leia and Ruth Ward, Georgina Barton and Louise Heringa; histories of Guelph, Fergus, Elora, Nichol, Puslinch and several church publications.

Here can be found also an original letter written in 1852 by Sir Isaac Pitman to William Buckingham, father of W. E. Buckingham, K.C.; letters to John D. Higinbotham from Oliver Wendell Holmes and Henry Van Dyke; from George Brown to A. E. Byerly; the original manuscript of "Old Guelph Fair,"[23] by Thomas Laidlaw; 1847 files of the *Herald* and the Coronation number of *The Mercury*; *Annals of the Town of Guelph* by C. Acton Burrows, the first known publication about Guelph from 1827 to 1877 and a diary kept by Lt.-Col. John

---

[10] Anne Sutherland Brooks wrote "Guelph - Our Heritage" for Guelph's Centennial in 1927 (Wiljer 1990:65).

[11] George Alexander Drew (1894-1973), elected Mayor of Guelph in 1925.

[12] Orlando John Stevenson wrote *The Lady of the Lake, With Annotations* (1915); *Shakespeare's Macbeth, With Annotations* (1916); *Seven Poems, With Annotations* (1930); *Hamlet, With Annotations* (1932).

[13] John D. Higinbotham grew up in Guelph and worked as a druggist, then moved to Lethbridge. He wrote *When the West Was Young: Historical Reminiscences of the Early Canadian West* (Toronto: Ryerson, 1933).

[14] Elinor Glyn wrote *'It': and other stories* (Duckworth, 1927).

[15] David Allan wrote *Some of Guelph's Old Landmarks* (Ontario Historical Society, 1934).

[16] See Appendix D.

[17] Scroggie was an alderman of Guelph in the late 1890's.

[18] Samuel Rupert Broadfoot wrote several poetry collections in the early 20th century, including *The Speed by Night* (1917).

[19] Maryan Beattie wrote *Jimney Cricket and Some Others* (T. H. Best, 1927).

[20] Mary Leslie (1843-1920). See Appendix D.

[21] Norman Guthrie had published three volumes of poetry by 1928.

[22] Laura Gertrude Lemon (1866-1924) was born in Guelph. She wrote music under her own name and lyrics under the names Austin Fleming and Ian Macdonald. Best remembered for "In Old Quebec" (1938).

[23] A copy of this Laidlaw poem is in the William Ready Division of Archives and Research Collections at McMaster University Library.

McCrae at sea on the way to the South African war; a map of British North American provinces and adjoining States, published in 1833.

The present collection focuses on the Guelph versifiers writing between 1827 and 1899. A literary critique of the works is left for future scholarship. Only versifiers are included in this collection; further investigation is encouraged into the prose and technical writers of the same period. Three examples will suffice. The explorer and author John McLean (c.1799-1890), who resided in Guelph from 1846 to 1857 at #21 Nottingham Street, and wrote under the pseudonym "Viator." David Kennedy, senior (1828-1903) died in Guelph,[24] and is noted for his *Incidents of Pioneer Days at Guelph and the County of Bruce* (Toronto, 1903). Likewise, as an item in the *Mercury* of 9 September, 1896, noted:

A very interesting paper, entitled 'Life Among The Lepers,' by Miss Lila Watt, B.A., Guelph, appears in the September number of 'The Westminster.'

Lila Watt published her sixteen-page paper, "European Lepers in India," in 1895. She lived at Sunny Acres, Guelph, and became the Secretary to The Mission to Lepers Society, Toronto, writing until 1908 when she began to suffer from ill health.

---

I do not necessarily share the sentiments expressed in the various verses in this collection, but I hope the reader will understand that these works reflect the very different social, political and religious context of 19th century Canada. Accepting this, I believe you will encounter surprising and enjoyable verses that express concepts that underlay the heritage of Guelph, Ontario, and Canada.

---

In order to prepare this collection, I have consulted various primary and secondary sources, including books, online scans of original publications and newspapers, and the wellspring to be found in the microfilm archives of the Guelph newspapers held at the Guelph Public Library (Main Branch). I am also indebted to enthusiastic personal communications with John Inglis' ancestors in Scotland, along with the helpful staff and resources at the University of Guelph Archival and Special Collections (McLaughlin Library). By consulting the Guelph newspaper archives it has been possible to include in this collection a number of forgotten versifiers, namely Thomas Murphy, "Fanny," "Jonathan," "Philo," R.B., John Pearson, Charles T. Daniel, Hetty Hazelwood, David Morrison, C. (Thornton), J.P.B., John Inglis, "Diogenes Redivivus," A.E.L. Treleaven, Charles C. Foster, "Madge," J.F.M., Anonymous Guelph Tourists, "Ricardo" and D.F.F. Nevertheless, I do not claim that this collection is completely comprehensive of all Guelph 19th century versifiers. Due to the unfortunate gaps in the newspaper archives, it would not be

---

[24] The Kennedy family emigrated to Canada and lived in Guelph from 1830 to 1851, in the Paisley Block on the homestead called Craigmorriston.

surprising that a number of now irretrievable verses have suffered extinction. Likewise, only those versifiers who wrote from, to or about Guelph are included. A future collection may include such fascinating figures as Emma Cripps, who flourished c.1900 in Eramosa Township.

This collection also does not include the extremely rare 24-page 1869 poem by Col. William Kingsmill (1794-1876), entitled "A Story of the Old Marine!"[25] Similarly, while Malcolm MacCormack[26] is known to have taught in Guelph, the dates of his poetic efforts are not clear.

The sections "Further Reading" and the seven appendices are intended as supplementary material on aspects of Guelph's 19th century culture of reading, writing and publishing. For the period 1827-1899, the appendices list and describe: Guelph's newspapers (Appendix A); Guelph's bookstores (Appendix B); Guelph's printers and bookbinders (Appendix C); Guelph libraries (Appendix D); books published in Guelph between the above dates (Appendix E); a note on Charles Julius Mickle, a Guelph settler who was the son of William Julius Mickle, a famous English poet (Appendix F); An anonymous local versifier and a response from Aberfoyle (Appendix G); a chronological list of Guelph versifiers in the same period (Appendix H).

To my best knowledge, this collection is the first of its kind for Guelph. A small unpublished handwritten manuscript by Hugh Douglass (c.1963) exists in the rare books collection of the Guelph Public Library (Main Branch), and an unsigned typed paper (c.1967) is in the rare books collection in the University of Guelph's McLaughlin Library. While both have examples of local poetry, they do not comprehensively explore the primary sources. Johnson (1977) also included a little information on the best known Guelph versifiers at the end of his book *History of Guelph 1827-1927*.[27] Beyond these, and a few noted articles published by the Guelph Historical Society, the present work is a significant comprehensive collection for general readership and literary scholars alike.

Therefore, in a celebratory gesture, I present this collection of works by Guelph versifiers of the 19th century. These are verses from, about, and for Guelph. Take up and read. Immerse yourself in a vibrant journey into the poesies of familiar and unfamiliar Guelph, a city unique for being made real by a writer of fiction. May you discover the intangible heritage of Guelph's writing and reading culture. May it act as a creative catalyst for present and future versifiers. And may Guelph's muse draw you to its fount of inspiration.

**DAVID J. KNIGHT**
General Editor - Vocamus Editions
Guelph, Ontario, Canada
2014

---

[25] The poem is mentioned by Wiljer (1990). See Appendix D. Kingsmill Avenue (Guelph) was named in 1913 after a relative- J.J. Kingsmill, a city solicitor (Irwin 1998:42).

[26] Clark 1900:233-235

[27] See Further Reading.

# I

# JOHN GALT

2 MAY, 1779, IRVINE, SCOTLAND -
11 APRIL, 1839, GREENOCK, SCOTLAND.
FOUNDED AND RESIDED IN GUELPH 1827-1829

To attempt a short biography of John Galt is like presenting a limited snapshot of an expansive labyrinth. To describe him simply as the founder, in 1827, of Guelph, in his official capacity as Secretary of the Canada Company, is to miss his literary endeavors. To focus only on the many novels which he wrote is to bypass his other artistic expressions. His interests were varied and broad. He made his own hurdy-gurdy; he was a playwright, a traveller, an entrepreneur, and biographer of friends Lord Byron (1788-1824) and painter Benjamin West (1738-1820). In present parlance, he was a social activist, being the Secretary in 1815 of the Royal Caledonian Asylum for Scottish Orphans in London.

John Galt is commemorated in Guelph with a 1979 bronze bust by John Miecznikowski outside the old City Hall and John Galt Public School on Laurine Avenue. Since 2006, Guelph celebrates the first Monday in August as "John Galt Day." In Greenock, Renfrewshire, Scotland, stands a John Galt memorial fountain on the Esplanade, and at the old cemetery where he is buried, a plaque remembers him. In Edinburgh, he is commemorated in Makar's Court, in the alley leading to The Writers' Museum, Lawnmarket.

When it comes to Galt's position as Guelph's first versifier, his poetic output in relation to his city foundation is sparse. The following poem entitled "Canadian Recollections," was written by Galt in May of 1837. While ailing near the end of an active life, at Greenock, Scotland, he may have been reminiscing about his sublime settlement in the heart of the 'impenetrable wilderness'[28]:

---

[28] "Canadian Recollections" also features in the Introduction to my new edition of John Galt's Gothic novel *The Omen* (Publication Studio Guelph, 2013).

## CANADIAN RECOLLECTIONS
(1837)

### I

At pensive eve, what time the sun
Peep'd through the trees, his journey done,
 I lov'd to walk the greenwood still,
 Where gloom seems silence visible,
 And note the fading hues of light,
 My heart partaking, too, of night.

### II

When flowers, that in the noonbeam shone
With colours like my hopes, were gone,
 Oft in the twilight of the wood,
 I own'd that aw'd prophetic mood,
 Which sees the future as a dream,
 And life a shadow'd woodland stream.

### III

Till through the boughs I chanced to see
The heavenly orb's bright revelry,
 And felt assured, however late,
 That time would be my advocate,
 And make my aims, despite my fear,
 As stars from darkness come, appear.

\*\*\*

# II

# $\mathfrak{S}$AMUEL $\mathfrak{S}$TRICKLAND

## 6 NOVEMBER, 1804, STOWE HOUSE, BUNGAY, SUFFOLK, ENGLAND - 3 JANUARY, 1867, LAKEFIELD, CANADA WEST (ONTARIO)

Samuel Strickland was a landowner, Canada Company official, and author. His father Thomas Strickland was manager of the Greenland Docks on the Thames, London. He retired and removed his family to Norwich, Norfolk. He rented Stowe House, and then in 1808 purchased Reydon Hall, an Elizabethan manor-house near Southwold on the Suffolk coast. Thomas died at Reydon Hall in May 1818.

Samuel's sisters were well known writers; Catharine (Parr Traill), Agnes and Susanna (Moodie). Catharine was a settler, author, teacher, and naturalist (9 January 1802 in Rotherhithe, London, England - 29 August 1899 at Lakefield, Ontario) and wrote *The tell tale: an original collection of moral and amusing stories* (anonymously, 1818); *The Backwoods of Canada...*(London, 1836) and *The Female Emigrant's Guide / The Canadian settler's guide* (Toronto, 1854 / 1855). Agnes was a well known English historical writer and poet. Susanna is most famous for her *Roughing it in the Bush* (1852) describing early Canadian pioneer life.

In 1825, Samuel Strickland immigrated to Darlington (Durham County). He married Emma Black. In May of 1826 he bought 200 acres of land in Douro Township near Peterborough. In 1828, John Galt employed Strickland as a Canada Company engineer and involved him in the development of Guelph.[29] Strickland was active in Guelph from 1828 to 1832. In 1828, Jehu Clarke is noted as building the bridge on the Eramosa Road and called it Strickland's Bridge.[30]

In 1853, Major Samuel Strickland, published his two volume *Twenty-seven years in Canada West: Or, The Experience of An Early Settler* (London, Richard Bentley). His sister Agnes Strickland (1796-1874) is acknowledged as the editor of the work, and noted as the "author of 'The Queens of England,' etc..".[31] Below the title of Volume I, Strickland in-

---

[29] *Dictionary of Canadian Biography.*

[30] "Death of an Old Settler" (obituary of Jehu Clarke); The *Mercury*, 1 August, 1879.

[31] Agnes Strickland wrote many children's books and historical biographies, including *Lives of the Queens of England*, in 12 volumes (1840-1848).

cluded the thirteenth stanza of his sister Agnes' poem "The Cottage Emigrants," from her *Historic Scenes and Poetic Fancies* (1850).[32] Here is the entire poem:

## THE COTTAGE EMIGRANTS

When yellow leaves were falling
        From every trembling spray,
I met three cottage children
        One bleak autumnal day.

They'd all day long been roaming
        Among the purple heath,
And plaited many a ferny crown,
        And many a harebell wreath.

They'd sung to every merry bird
        That gaily flitted by,
And chased upon his lonely flight
        The year's last butterfly.

They'd drank the crystal waters
        Of many a gushing spring,
And blithely traced with jocund feet
        The fairies' emerald ring.

To them the bramble yielded
        Refreshment by the way,
When they cull'd its luscious treasure,
        And the hawthorn's coral spray.

And often as they rested
        On rustic stile or rail,
They artlessly recounted
        Some pretty childish tale.

---

[32] *Historic Scenes and Poetic Fancies* by Agnes Strickland. London: Henry Colburn 1850. Printed in London by Savill and Edwards, 4, Chandos Street, Covent Garden. Agnes wrote *Historic Scenes* from the Strickland home - Reydon Hall, Suffolk, England.

'Twas pleasant, in my lonely walks,
  To meet that loving train;
But now, at morn or eventide,
  I look for them in vain.

Stern Want has rudely forced them
  With exiled bands to roam,
To seek in distant lands the bread
  They could not win at home.

And soon their native England,
  And Suffolk's verdant vales,
Will seem like dreamy memories,
  Or scenes in fairy tales.

But brighter hopes shall greet them
  Amidst the pathless wild,
Than e'er on Britain's cultured soil
  For British peasants smiled.

The hands that wove the useless flowers
  Are called the sheaves to bind,
While golden harvests of their own
  The sons of labour find.

The children's faces brighten
  Around the evening blaze,
While Industry forgets the toils
  Of busy, well-spent days.

And when those toils rewarding,
  Broad lands at length they'll claim,
They'll call the new possession
  By some familiar name.

> The name beyond all others,
> Endeared in grief or mirth,
> Of that far-distant village
> Which gave the exiles birth.[33]

## "THE APPALLING WHIRLWIND: GUELPH, 1829"

While in Guelph, Samuel Strickland was witness, in May of 1829, to what he described as an "appalling whirlwind" that swept through the two-year-old town. He proposed that since "it appears very evident that storms of this description have not been unfrequent in the wooded regions of Canada; and it becomes a matter of interesting consideration, whether the clearing of our immense forests will not, in a great measure, remove the cause of these phenomena."[34] He composed verse about this tornado and had it published in 1848, noting in his *Twenty-seven years* (1853) "My description of this whirlwind, and the accompanying lines, have already appeared in the 'Victoria Magazine,'"[35] published in Canada West, under the signature of "Pioneer."[36] His verses on the 1829 tornado that swept through Guelph can be considered the earliest verse to be composed at Guelph, about Guelph.

"I witnessed the most appalling land tornado (if so I may term it), I ever saw in my life. As this is a phenomenon seldom if ever witnessed in England, I think a particular description may possibly interest those readers who are unaccustomed to such eccentricities of Nature.

In my hunting excursions and rambles through the Upper Canadian forests, I had frequently met with extensive windfalls; and observed with some surprise that the fallen trees appeared to have been twisted off at the stumps, for they lay strewn in a succession of circles. I also remarked, that these windfalls were generally narrow, and had the appearance of a wide road slashed through the forest.

---

[33] Agnes Strickland 1850:394-396

[34] Strickland 1853:245. Another severe tornado hit the north and east borders of Guelph in August of 1868 (see *Evening Mercury* 1 September, 1868).

[35] *The Victoria Magazine* 1847-1848, Volume 1, page 101. For one year, from September 1847 to August 1848, Samuel Strickland's sister Susanna and her husband John Wedderburn Dunbar Moodie, edited *The Victoria Magazine* for Joseph Wilson of Belleville. "They wrote much of the material themselves and received contributions from her siblings Catharine, Samuel, and Agnes" (Poetry Foundation entry for Susanna Moodie). An advertisement for the *Victoria Magazine*, "edited by Mr and Mrs Moodie" appeared in the *Guelph & Galt Advertiser* (24 August, 1848).

[36] Strickland 1853:243;246. Also cited in Burrows' 1877 *Annals of Guelph* (page 45), see Further Reading.

From observations made at the time, and since confirmed, I have no doubt Colonel Reid's theory of storms[37] is a correct one, viz. : - 'That all windstorms move in a circular direction, and the nearer the centre, the more violent the wind.' Having seen the effects of several similar hurricanes since my residence in Canada West, I shall describe one which happened in the township of Guelph, during the early part of the summer of 1829.

The weather, for the season of the year (May) had been hot and sultry, with scarcely a breath of wind stirring. I had heard distant thunder from an early hour of the morning, which from the eastward is rather an unusual occurrence. About ten A.M. the sky had a most singular, I may say, a most awful appearance; presenting to the view a vast arch of rolling blackness, which seemed to gather strength and density as it approached the zenith. All at once the clouds began to work round in circles, as if chasing one another through the air. Suddenly, the dark arch of clouds appeared to break up into detached masses, whirling and eddying through each other in dreadful commotion. The forked lightning was incessant, accompanied by heavy thunder. In a short space the clouds seemed to converge to a point, which approached very near the earth, still whirling with great rapidity directly under this point; and apparently from the midst of the woods arose a black column in the shape of a cone, which instantly joined itself to the depending cloud: the sight was now grand and awful in the extreme.

Let any one picture to the imagination a vast column of smoke of inky blackness reaching from earth to heaven, gyrating with fearful velocity; bright lightnings issuing from the vortex - the roar of the thunder - the rushing of the blast - the crashing of timber, mingled with clouds of dust, whirling through the air - a faint idea is then given of the scene.

> Through all the sky arise outrageous storms,
> And death stands threatening in a thousand forms;
> Clouds charged with loud destruction drown the day,
> And airy demons in wild whirlwind play;
> Thick thunderclaps, and lightning's vivid glare
> Disturb the sky, and trouble all the air.

I had ample time for observation as the hurricane commenced its desolate course about two miles from the town, through the centre of which it took its way, passing within fifty yards of the spot where a number of persons and myself were standing watching its fearful progress. As the tornado approached, the trees seemed to fall like a pack of cards before its irresistible current. After passing through the clearing made around the town, the force of the wind gradually abated. and in a few minutes died away entirely.

---

[37] Sir William Reid (1791-1858) directed the reconstruction after the Great Barbados hurricane of 1831, when he studied tropical storms and published *An Attempt to Develop the Law of Storms by Means of Facts* (1838) and *The Progress of the Development of the Law of Storms and of the Variable Winds* (1849).

As soon as the storm was over, I went to see what damage it had done. From the point where I first observed the black column to rise from the woods and join the cloud, the trees were twisted in every direction. A belt of timber had been levelled to the ground about two miles in length, and about one hundred yards in breadth: at the entrance of the town it crossed the river Speed, and up-rooted about six acres of wood which had been thinned out and left by Mr. Galt as an ornament to his house[38].

The Eremosa road[39] was completely blocked up for nearly half a mile, in the wildest confusion possible. In its progress through the town, it unroofed several houses, levelled the fences to the ground, and entirely demolished a frame-barn: windows were dashed in, and in one instance the floor of a log-house was carried up through the roof. Some hair-breadth escapes occurred, but, luckily, no lives were lost."[40]

> Dark, heavy clouds were gathering in the west,
>> Wrapping the forest in funereal gloom;
> Onward they roll'd and rear'd each livid crest,
>> Like death's murk shadows frowning o'er earth's tomb:
> From out the inky womb of that deep night
>> Burst livid flashes of electric flame:
> Whirling and circling with terrific might,
>> In wild confusion on the tempest came.
> Nature, awakening from her still repose,
>> Shudders responsive to the whirlwind's shock
> Feels at her mighty heart convulsive throes;
>> Her groaning forests to earth's bosom rock.
> But, hark! what means that hollow rushing sound,
>> That breaks the sudden stillness of the morn?
> Red forked lightnings fiercely glare around:
>> What crashing thunders on the winds are borne!
> And see you spiral column, black as night,
>> Rearing triumphantly its wreathing form;
> Ruin's abroad, and through the murky light,
>> Drear desolation marks the spirit of the storm.

* * * * * * * *

---

[38] Galt's house in Guelph became known as The Priory, formerly on what is now Woolwich Street, near Allan's Bridge.

[39] More usually known as Eramosa Road.

[40] Strickland 1853:241-244

How changed the scene; the awful tempest's o'er;
From dread array and elemental war
The lightning's flash hath ceased, the thunder's roar -
The glorious sun resumes his golden car.[41]

## WORKS:

Samuel Strickland's verses on the 1829 Guelph tornado are in *The Victoria Magazine* 1847-1848, Volume 1, page 101.

Samuel Strickland 1853. *Twenty-seven years in Canada West: Or, The Experience of An Early Settler*, in two volumes. London: Richard Bentley, New Burlington Street, and printed by Samuel Bentley & Co. Bangor House, Shoe Lane.

\*\*\*

---

[41] Strickland 1853:245-246

# III

## JOHN TAYLOR

### FLOURISHED 1836

John Taylor was the original settler on Lot 13, Concession 1, Division B, Guelph Township.[42] Taylor composed new verses to be sung to the music of "The Wearing of the Green"[43] on 4 October, 1836. His poem is entitled "The Paisley Block Ball":

### PAISLEY BLOCK BALL

(4 October, 1836. Reprinted in the *Guelph Evening Mercury* 20 July, 1927)

Think of Great Columbus, that man of worth and fame,
Who found out this great continent that should have borne his name.
In his voyage of discovery no dangers did appal,
Or we might not now be singing at a Paisley Block Ball.

*Chorus* -   At a Paisley Block Ball,
At a Paisley Block Ball,
Or we might not now be singing
At a Paisley Block Ball.

Our old Mother Country, the land of the brave,
So deeply sunk in debt, the sponge can only save;
The thought of a civil war we did not like at all,
For fighting's not so pleasant as a Paisley Block Ball.

---

[42] Johnson (1977:334). Johnson suggests Taylor's poem is 'perhaps the first poem composed in the Guelph area" (*Ibid.*), although Strickland's versified description of the tornado of 1829 (see above) is a more obvious candidate.

[43] "'The Wearing of the Green' is an Irish street ballad lamenting the repression of supporters of the Irish Rebellion of 1798. It is an old Irish air, and many versions of the lyrics exist." (Wikipedia article: *The Wearing of the Green*).

*Chorus -* At a Paisley Block Ball,
At a Paisley Block Ball,
For fighting's not so pleasant
At a Paisley Block Ball.

So we left our native land and those we dearly love,
The tears did flow in torrents, while the vessel off did move;
We trusted to the ocean, whatever did befall,
So here we are rejoicing at a Paisley Block Ball.

*Chorus -* At a Paisley Block Ball,
At a Paisley Block Ball,
So here we are rejoicing
At a Paisley Block Ball.

Our friends and relations that we did leave behind,
Relief from their burdens we hope they soon will find;
That they are happy, we wish them one and all,
We are here with mirth and glee at the Paisley Block Ball.

*Chorus -* At a Paisley Block Ball,
At a Paisley Block Ball,
As we are here with mirth and glee
At the Paisley Block Ball.

When we came to the wild land all covered with wood,
We soon made a clearance where mighty timber stood;
By steady perseverance, we made many a tree to fall,
Which led us on to comforts and a Paisley Block Ball.

*Chorus -* And a Paisley Block Ball,
And a Paisley Block Ball,
Which led us on to comforts
And a Paisley Block Ball.

Now to the ladies, the partners of our lives,
We wish every comfort to sweethearts and wives;
They're like as many stars all shining in the hall,
And move about most gracefully at the Paisley Block Ball.

*Chorus -*      At a Paisley Block Ball,
                At a Paisley Block Ball,
                And move about most gracefully
                At the Paisley Block Ball.

From all the ills of life, we wish they may be free,
Without them the place a wilderness would be,
We'll drink to the ladies' healths, I know you join me shall,
For their beauty is the lustre of the Paisley Block Ball.

*Chorus -*      Of the Paisley Block Ball,
                Of the Paisley Block Ball,
                For their beauty is the lustre
                Of the Paisley Block Ball.

We have horses, cows and pigs, we have poultry and sheep,
We have produce for to sell and plenty still to keep;
We have instruments to cut, and cattle for to haul,
So we'll toast our noble selves at the Paisley Block Ball.

*Chorus -*      At a Paisley Block Ball,
                At a Paisley Block Ball,
                So we'll toast our noble selves
                At the Paisley Block Ball.

Now to conclude, your patience I will praise,
And thank you for your chorus unto my humble lays;
Though my song it be but homespun, and but a silly scrawl,
It may set wiser heads to work for next Paisley Block Ball.

*Chorus -*      For next Paisley Block Ball,
                For next Paisley Block Ball,
                It may set wiser heads to work
                For next Paisley Block Ball.

\*\*\*

# IV

## 𝕿HOMAS 𝕸URPHY

**FLOURISHED 1846**

Thomas Murphy owned a farmstead in Guelph Township formerly called the Dwyer Farm[44]. His son John Murphy worked the farm, and by 1877 it was known as Mount Tara, in reference to the Hill of Tara,[45] near the River Boyne in County Meath, Ireland, traditionally believed to be the seat of the high-kings of Ireland. John Murphy appealed to the *Mercury* to print his father's poem, originally composed in response to the Great Famine of Ireland (1845-1849). The poem was printed in the *Mercury* on 28 January, 1880, in response to the Irish famine of 1879.

### LINES ON THE APPROACHING FAMINE
### OF 1846-47 IN IRELAND
(September 1846; printed in the *Daily Mercury* 28 January, 1880)

The following lines have been sent us for publication. They were composed by the late Thomas Murphy, father of Mr John Murphy, of Mount Tara, Guelph Township. They depict in forcible language the miseries of that terrible period:-

> Hark! dearest Island, afflicted for ages,
> > The victim of famine, oppression and grief
> That moistens the eyes of your historic pages,
> > The spot is scarce met, that treats of relief.
> > > Now ruin's black mantle in sorrow hangs o'er you,
> > > With pestilence raging and famine before you,
> > > That oppresses the feelings of those that adore you;
> > > Thy woes are increasing, sweet land of the brave.

---

[44] See Thompson 1877 (Further Reading).

[45] Known in Irish as *Cnoc na Teamhrach, Teamhair* or *Teamhair na Rí*.

How sad must thy fields look though spangled with flowers,
     When eyes dimm'd with famine behold you with pain.
Whilst hunger increases and pestilence lowers,
     And death mowing down where there's naught to sustain.
          To beg is in vain, for all tell the same story -
          The infant expiring, the youthful and hoary -
          Prostrated in prayer, to the God of all glory
          They call out despairing and yet call in vain.

Despair's darkling round like a cloud fraught with venom,
     Corroding the vitals that famine subdued,
And the ports by fierce tyrants are closed up 'gainst them
     Which leaves them to linger and famish for food.
          The fireside mirth and the glance of the lover -
          The songs of the Bards and the tales of the rover,
          And thy heart melting friendship dear Erin is over,
          For the hand clasping Cead mille failthe[46] is gone.

The dim sunken eyes of the pale, grieving mother
     Are wasted with tears o'er her long stinted brood:
In vain is the soothing no language can smother,
     They cry out like spectres still asking for food.
          Alas! they complain she has naught left to give them,
          Nor no distant prospect of hopes to relieve them;
          They cry till they sleep, but the morning deceives them,
          The evening's complaints are still feebly renewed.

The strong man is weak, and his sight is declining,
     The bold and aspiring move deviously on -
All blight'd by hunger, disease and repining,
     And the rose blooming cheeks of your daughters are wan.
          How sour are the dregs of the gall they are tasting,
          Whilst revelling tyrants sit sumptuous wasting,
          And the spoils of distress they are wantonly wasting,
          Nor deal out the crumbs to the widow's last groan.

---

[46] Irish Gaelic: *céad míle fáilte* = "a hundred thousand welcomes."

The graves of our fathers won't long be forsaken,
  Whilst the waves of disease floats down to the tomb
And no feeble gleam through the darkness is breaking -
  The black thickening cloud of distress to illume.
      The shamrock is seared and the flowerets are fading,
      Through floods of distress the pale victims are wending,
      Though sympathy's arm is now stretch'd to aid them -
      Still thousands of brave ones are gone to the tomb.

Though far from the land of my youth and ambition,
  My spirit steals back to your home with a sigh
That melts through the heart at your awful condition,
  And forces those tears that fall hot from the eye.
      Of solace bereav'd we can only condole you -
      Our mite we have gain'd with a hope to console you
      And wish you were here with our friends to enrole you
      'Midst plenty to live and contentedly die.

* * *

# V

## James McGrogan

**FLOURISHED 1847**

The life and career of James McGrogan is obscure, other than what may be gleaned from his poem written for the Guelph *Herald* in 1847. His mother was Elizabeth McGrogan and apparently buried in "Cranfield tomb."

### Lines Written On The Death Of Elizabeth McGrogan, By Her Son, James.

("Written for the Guelph Herald" Printed in the *Herald* 12 October, 1847)

> O, cruel Death what hast thou done,
> Why wast thou so severe;
> Oh! why so soon her glass was run,
> My tender mother dear.
>
> She nurtur'd me when I was young,
> But now she is no more;
> From her to many estates I sprung,
> Then must I not deplore.
>
> For nature binds the human heart,
> And I must here repine;
> From my dear mother I must part,
> She'll be no longer mine.
>
> Her children dear must weep and wail,
> They lost a mother kind;
> But on her grave they'll shed a tear,
> For nature does them bind.

But still there is a heavenly hope,
 Her soul is soar'd above;
There to enjoy the boundless scope
 Of Christ's redeeming love.

In whose redemption made complete,
 She'll join the mighty throng;
Where ransom'd Jew and Gentile meet,
 To sing Salvation's song.

Then let us cease to heave a sigh,
 Though death did sternly call;
But trust her Spirit reigns on high,
 Where God is all in all.

That hope shall make us cease to mourn,
 For why should we despair;
To earth our mother won't return,
 But we shall meet her there.

But still her mould'ring dust must lie,
 Enclosed in Cranfield tomb;
Till judgment seals in yonder sky,
 Her last eternal doom.

\*\*\*

# VI

## 𝕲eorge 𝕻irie

**28 February, 1799, Aberdeen, Scotland -
22 July, 1870, Guelph, Canada**

George Pirie[47] was the proprietor of the *Guelph Herald* newspaper 1848-1870 (see Appendix A on Guelph newspapers). His relative was Sir John Pirie (1781-1851), Lord Mayor of London (1841-42).[48] George Pirie was secretary of the St. Andrew's Society in Guelph for 21 years (1849-1870), and has been remembered in *Selections from Scottish Canadian Poets* (1900).[49] His obituary appeared in the *Guelph Herald* on 27 July, 1870, and he is buried in Woodlawn Cemetery, Guelph. Pirie's private and unpublished papers included some romantic poems, and poems relating to death and mourning. A selection of his poems were published in pamphlet form by the *Guelph Herald* as "Lyrics of the Late George Pirie, Esq." (1870). Much of his writing was lost in a house fire, although a booklet of handwritten unpublished poetry, primarily romantic, has been preserved.[50]

### THE REFORMED CROWS

(Printed in the Guelph *Herald* 2 November, 1847)

Whoe'er has heard of Illinois,
But knows how in that State the Crow is
    In seed-time, quite a huge annoyance;
Exacting then his tithe as duly,
As if he knew the season truly,
    By what the learned call "clair voyance."

---

[47] A full biographical treatment of George Pirie is available on Wikipedia.

[48] Burrows 1877:147-148

[49] Clark 1900:129

[50] Wikipedia article on George Pirie.

A farmer in that land of prairie,
Had planted out his field quite early,
　　Thus hoping to escape detection;
But scarcely was his corn covered,
When o'er his head a legion hovered,
　　Resolved on personal inspection.

With voice and rifle as he might,
He cheered, and charged them, left and right,
　　Their number grew the more enormous.
They cawed, they scratched, they hopped, they fed,
'Troy Warren' wings, waved o'er his head,
　　Quite a-la-mode 'Cornelius Corvus.'

Our friend now almost in despair,
Bethought him of a 'ruse de guerre,'
　　And set about it on the spot.
Some grain he steeps in Alcohol,
Then up and out, and sows the whole,
　　Try broad-cast o'er his corn plot.

The felon crows with stomachs empty,
Rejoice amid the unlooked for plenty;
　　The bait is swallowed in a chatter.
But soon each rogue begins to feel,
So very queer from head to heel,
　　He wonders what can be the matter.

The steam is up - a polka ho!
They hop, they skip, they jump 'Jim Crow,'
　　Like other bipeds in their glory;
'All hands aloft!' up, up, oh, rare,
They're somerseting in the air,
　　All cawing, screaming, 'con-a-more.'

Behold them now in sober mood,
High perched within a neighbouring wood,
 Discussing of their doings errant;
Through hole they argued the affair,
It boots not that the muse declare,
 But the result was soon apparent.

On every patch of corn round,
The crows by hundreds still were found,
 Unchanged in habits or appearance.
(We don't pretend that birds have reason,)
Yet not a crow through all that season,
 Re-visited our farmer's clearance.

## THE SONG OF THE SEWING MACHINE

(Printed in 1870: "Lyrics By The Late George Pirie, Esq.")

Tom Hood made the world to sigh,
 When the "Song of the Shirt" was his theme,
I doubt if there's many will cry,
 O'er the song of the Sewing Machine.
Alas! for the poor white slave,
 In poverty, hunger and dirt,
Who sung as she made, with a double thread,
 A shroud, as well as a shirt!

 Stitch ! Stitch ! Stitch !
When the sun was unclouded and bright,
 And stitch-stitch-stitch,
When the lamps on the street were alight,
 Seam and gusset and band,
 Band and gusset and seam,
The graveyard was fed by the needle and thread,
 'Ere the birth of the Sewing Machine.

Whir ! Whir ! Whir !
A change in the music - hurrah !
Whir ! Whir ! Whir !
The Sewing Machine's under way,
Beam and shuttle and wheel,
Wheel and shuttle and beam,
And the needles, my eye, how the fairy things fly,
And the linen runs off in a stream.

Work ! work ! work !
As spry as a 2.20 team,
And work-work-work,
As if the thing went by steam;
And you look for the boiler below,
But that only shows you are green,
For the hand of a girl, or the toe,
Is the power of the Sewing Machine,

Work ! work ! work !
It works without waiting to talk,
It never gets sleepy nor sick,
And it never goes out for a walk.
It's teetotal record is clear;
It never fails fast days to keep:
Nor grumbles, how cheer, that bread is so dear,
While Sewing Machines are so cheap.

O ! maids who have chamises to seam,
O ! men who makes trews *a la Turk*,
Come see how this little machine,
Will save you a world of work.
Have done with your sewing by hand,
It makes you both languid and lean,
If you wish to get wealth and to husband your health,
You must purchase a sewing machine !

You would know where these marvels are made,
    In the good Town of Guelph I reply;
And though thousands are sold, it is said
    The demand is beyond the supply.
      Whir-whir-whir.
    A rude little minstrel I ween,
Yet more cheerful by far than of lute or guitar
    Is the voice of the Sewing Machine.


## THE SINGING-BIRDS

(Printed in the Herald 31 July, 1866:
"Prelude for Mr. Youman's Next Juvenile Concert - By the Editor."
Printed again in 1870: "Lyrics By The Late George Pirie, Esq.")

We come to tarn your thoughts awhile
    From politics and pelf;
To bring you proof that we've struck "ile"
    At singing school in Guelph.

Chorus.
Oh, love your little singing-birds,
    Throw sunshine o'er the throng;
The noon may mar with wailing words
    Their merry morning song.

No bevy of fair foreign birds,
    No nightingales are we,
To witch your eyes with gorgeous dyes,
    Your hearts with melody.

We're just such little warbling things
    As May-day wakes to sing;
No winter yet has warped our wings,
    We've known no time but spring.

We meekly for your favor sue,
    Mind we're but young and shy;
We're going to sing "Red, White and Blue,"
    And "Comin' thro' the Rye."

And "I'm o'er young to marry yet,"
    And songs with stirring words,
And every "Pa" who owns a pet
    Will cheer the singing-birds.

We're freedom's fledglings, forest bred;
    If caged we couldn't sing.
We dare a foeman's hand to shred
    A feather from our wing!

We have no fears, our volunteers,
    Again should raiders roam,
Will not forget when foes are met,
    Their singing birds at home.

### FAR FROM CLAN ALPINE DHU

(Printed in 1870: "Lyrics By The Late George Pirie, Esq.")

Far from Clan Alpine Dhu,
Wanders the bonnet blue;
Still to that magnet true,
Turns his heart thither.
Far though his fate may part,
Land of his love thou art,
Ever the Scottish heart
Warms to the heather.

## THE EMIGRANT'S RETURN

("By the Editor of the Guelph Herald" Printed 11 February, 1851)

There's a glen by the Gairn, a valley on Dee,
Than the "Vale of Avoca" 'tis dearer to me;
Where the rush of the linn is in every ravine,
And the birch hangs her tassels o'er fountain and stream.
And the bleak Lochnagar, in his mantle of snow,
Looks down on the rocks and the rivers below.
From the crest of that mountain my eye first looked forth
On the green waves that girdle the shores of the north;
And they told me that, far o'er that fathomless main,
Was the land whence the gold and the emerald came;
And I deemed that the cloud in its vapoury fold,
As it glowed in the east, was that island of gold;
And I longed, when the cuckoo was pond'ring her flight,
To go forth with her then to that region of lght.
I turned to the valley, but there was alone,
The fane where I worshipp'd, the glory was gone.

I have looked upon mountains more mighty by far
Than the proud peaks that gather around Lochnagar,
And my bark has been bounding o'er waters that be
As the wave of the ocean to that of the Dee.
I have stood in the midst of the land of my dreams.
There are gems in the mountains, and gold in the streams;
And the heavens around it are cloudless and bright,
A glory by day and a halo by night;
And Earth yields her harvests, and Ocean her spoil,
Unsadden'd by sorrow, untarnish'd by toil;
And strange birds are there, in their gorgeous dyes,
That like winged flowers float in these balmy skies;
And fountains are flashing, and rivers of song
Are glancing and gliding the valleys along.
Oh! who that the bliss of such fair land might claim,
Would sigh to go over the wild waves again?

They have built me a bower in the valley so fair,
They have called it my home, - but my heart is not there;
There are things to *admire*, but to *love* there are none;
The land may be *Eden* - it is not my *home*.
Once more on the billow - yet not as before,
For the rush of the east wind gives rapture no more;
Yet the sail of my galley is spreading as wide,
And fleet as of yore she bounds over the tide.
Oh! fair must the isle be, and flowery and bright,
That will win her to linger an hour in her flight
Away o'er the waters ! away for the land
Where the giant St. Kilda does sentinel stand!
And the prow of my bark is again on the shore,
And I look on the mountains that look on Dalmore.
I turn from the ocean to kneel by the Dee,
And to vow there's no land like 'my ain countrie.'

## A Song For The Times
(By "S.T.T." = George Pirie. Printed in the *Guelph Herald* 7 January, 1851)

Wee Johnnie S---[51] cam' to our town,
  A *muckle* sheet to print:
Resolved, whatever it might cost
  That he wad swell his mint.

The paper and the types were got,
  The rollers and the press
But what to write, or what to print,
  Wee Johnnie couldna guess.

He didna wish to gie offence
  To either Rad or Tory.
Because the loss of *either*'s pence
  Wad mak' him very sorry.

---

[51] Johnson (1977) notes that this and John Smith's ("wee Johnnie" in Pirie's poem) rebuttal poem "were part of a lengthy exchange between George Pirie, editor of the *Guelph Herald* and John Smith, editor of the Guelph *Advertiser*...as a result of Smith's reply to 'A Song for the Times' Pirie challenged Smith to a duel." (1977:336).

When Johnnie asked the Tory lads
    If they would buy his paper,
No party man was he at all
    No *enemy* to "Draper."

His winning manner, witching words
    And smirking bonnie face
Made honest folk believe wee John
    Could not be a "hard case."

He hadna printed very long
    Before his greed of pelf
Was visible, and folks began
    To watch the little elf.

He tried to please both parties weel
    Wi' soft soap editorial
(Which mongrel "loose fish" politics
    Are Johnnie's sad memorial.)

The Tories they wad not be gull'd
    (Those sly discerning lads, )
And Johnnie, as a last resource,
    Cried, "Hurrah for the Rads!"

Puir simple souls, they took the bait -
    And Johnnie then began
In vanity and self-deceit
    To set up for a MAN!!!

Unsparingly he plied the taws
    To simple Austin's back[52],
Till "Liberals" were satisfied
    Wee Johnnie was no quack.

---

[52] Johnson notes: "Austin was the first editor of the Herald" (1977:337).

The scene it changed! a sick'ning change
　　Which made his prospects eerie
As henceforth he wad have to fight
　　Wi' far-famed "Poor old Pirie."

He struggled hard - wi' *foreign aid*
　　His page was often fired,
Till quite unequal to the task,
　　He POMPOUSLY retired.

Determined that he'd ne'er oppose
　　What's the prevailing passion,
(Even Johnnie was a Temperance man
　　Where that was a' the fashion.)

Did Johnnie, wi' his press and types
　　E'er rectify abuses?
We answer, NO! But then - but then -
　　*He biggit twa bra houses*!

*Postscript*
His mantle, it has fall'n on one
　　Wha at the Fates did fret
Because a single *liberal* type
　　His fingers never set.

Deplorable condition this
　　For any "man of feeling,"
If you'd be happy, "cut and run"
　　I pray thee, G.M.K.---g![53]

**WORKS:**

George Pirie 1870. *Lyrics By The Late George Pirie, Esq., For Twenty-Two Years Editor and Proprietor of the Guelph Herald*. Guelph: Printed at the Herald Book and Job Printing Establishment.

---

[53] Johnson notes: "G.M. Keeling, temporarily editor of the *Advertiser* and founding editor of the *Mercury*" (1977:337). See the next section (VII), for John ("Johnnie") Smith's versified rebuttal.

Included in this collection are earlier poems that Pirie had printed in the *Herald*, including:
"The Reformed Crows" (printed in the Guelph *Herald* 2 November, 1847)
"The Son Of Temperance" (In the Guelph *Herald* 7 January, 1851)
"The Emigrant's Return" (In the Guelph *Herald* 11 February, 1851)
"Bonny Mary Graeme" (In the Guelph *Herald* 25 February, 1851)
"The Singing-Birds" (In the Guelph *Herald* 31 July, 1866)

\*\*\*

# VII

## 𝕵OHN 𝕾MITH

### 1818, BOW HATHERNE, LEICESTERSHIRE, ENGLAND - 1899, GUELPH

John Smith established the *Guelph & Galt Advertiser* (later, called the *Guelph Advertiser*) newspaper in 1844. Smith was elected Guelph's first Mayor in 1856, and Councillor of the West Ward, until his defeat at the polls in 1857, to George Sunley. Smith may have been behind a political poem appearing in this paper entitled "A New Song," on 18 July, 1849, and signed: "NOT by the Editor of the Herald," i.e. contrary to George Pirie (section VI). In 1851, following George Pirie's scathing libelous poem ("A Song For The Times"), Smith replied two days later with "Another Song For The Times,"[54] as though it were written by Pirie's mother. It is evident the two men disliked each other, and yet the versified battle between them is fascinating.

### ANOTHER SONG FOR THE TIMES
("Written after reading the 'Song for the times' published in last '*Herald*'";
Printed in the Guelph *Advertiser* 9 January, 1851)

When Georgie P---e cam' to town
A *muckle* sheet to print;
Resolved, if possible, that he'd
Recruit his bankrupt "mint,"

Some paper and some types were got.
An *tick*, as you may guess,
An straightway Georgie cam' to be
A "gemman of the Press."

---

[54] Johnson 1977:337-338

Now, how to write or how to print,
    Poor Georgie did not know;
So off he went to old friend John,
    To ask him what to do.

Said John, "You shouldna gie offence
    To either Rad or Tory,
Be very smooth to one and all -
    To saints - or sinners hoary;

And when you "write," you should *uphold*
    The *Honor* of your Order, -
Be bland to all, and keep on hand
    Plenty of good soft-sawder.

And then your principles, - if any
    Principles you've got -
Keep shady - bottle them - or pr'aps
    Your types may go to pot.

Soap everybody - that's the way
    To catch the people's pence;
If e'er you *speak your mind* you're sure
    To give some sad offence.

Well Georgie went to work, but soon
    His precious greed o'pelf
Spoiled all the sawder that he gave
    To others or himself;

He tried to please all parties weel
    Wi' soft soap editorial
And mongrel "loose fish" politics,
    Stale and undignitorial;

He soaped the folks, and many gull'd
    With finely - and cooked up stories
'Bout how he'd put the taverns down
    And whip'd some drunken Tories, -

Puir simple souls, they took the bait,
    And Georgie then began
In vanitie and "self-consate"
    To set up for a *Man!*

Not only *that*, he set up for
    The first Reeve's chair to fill[55] -
But gosh! - that's slipped him, and he's had
    To gulp a bitter pill!

His hopes were at the top o' the poll,
    Which made him blithe and cheery;
But now they're smashed, and he's no *Reeve*
    Nor aught but *"Poor old Pirie."*

*Postscript*
Dear "Advertiser" now I've got
    Some good advice to give, -
Stand by your *colours* and your *friends*
    As long as you shall live;

Your chosen banner keep unfurl'd,
    Stick to it to the last;
And IF it e'er in danger be,
    Nail, NAIL IT TO THE MAST!

But *danger*! lor! you've no stern foe
    To meet in contest weary;
Your foe he's not a *Man* - What then?
    Why, he is POOR OLD PIRIE!

Never deny your colours like
    That poor old coon has done;
But to 'em stick, - and we'll yet see
    That covy "cut and run."

                          By S.T.T.'s Mother

\*\*\*

---

[55] The first post of Guelph Reeve went instead to Samuel Smith in 1851 (Johnson 1977:363).

# VIII

## 𝔉rances ("𝔉anny")

**Flourished 1847; Nichol County, Ontario**

All that is known of Frances ("Fanny") is that she resided in Nichol County and regularly wrote verse for the Guelph *Herald* during the year 1847. Her surname and career remains unknown. At the time when she was writing verses for the Guelph *Herald*, this newspaper was run by George Pirie, who, also in 1847, resided at Maryville in Nichol County. Therefore, Frances may be a relative of Pirie. Her verses from the Guelph *Herald* include:

### [Fragment: Title unknown]
(submitted to the Guelph *Herald* 9 August, 1847; printed 26 August, 1847)

> ...,
> From rival friendship flee away,
> Else virtue's blasted in a day.
> True friendship dwells in every breast,
> Where virtue in undisputed away,
> Bids the glad heart its voice obey.
> Where God's own image is enshrined,
> There, friendship thou wilt ever find.

### Thoughts Upon Seeing An Ivy Spreading Its Foliage Around The Stump Of An Oak
(submitted 20 August, 1847; printed 2 September, 1847)

#### I

> Loud roared the wind, the lightning flashed,
> And deaf'ning pealed the thunder;
> The angry waves the bold shore lashed,
> And man looked on in wonder.

## II

The sturdy oak, first bowed, then crashed,
Before God's mighty power;
Midway from roots to branch it smashed,
And left a graceless tower.

## III

The clinging ivy drooped and pined;
Its stay was now no more,
For years that lofty oak entwined,
And Heavenward did soar.

## IV

Oh, hapless fate! God's dread command,
Hath laid these low in dust;
E'en so He'll touch with with'ring hand,
This world of sin and lust.

## V

The Ivy mounts the rugged stump again,
And this its cheerful song:
"My leaves shall deck thee o'er, and I the same
"Will choose thee from the throng
"On which to aspire to joys above this earth;
"'Tis mine the privilege to choose,
"Of other trees more fortunate in birth,
"To bind them to my views."

## VI

"But Thee, I cannot now forsake,
"Amidst thy hopeless sorrow;
"My smiling vines, a screen shall make,
"That loftier trees would borrow."

## VII

That rugged Oak, that cheerful vine,
Are types of Mortals human;
The Oak is man, in sturdy prime,
The Vine, the loving Woman.

### TO CAROLINE

(submitted 28 August, 1847; printed 9 September, 1847)

A graceful form and lovely mien,
A damask cheek and dark blue eye,
The thoughtless mind may treasures deem,
Which fools, at dearest cost may buy.

But what are beauties of the face,
The ruby lip, and dimpled chin,
Unless combined with mental grace,
And moral worth combined within?

O, prize not then those trifling toys
Which have no charm in Wisdom's eye;
Which only yield unstable joys,
That with the fleeting moments fly.

But strive, oh, early strive, to find
Those precious gems which fadeless prove;
Which while on earth adorn the mind,
And brighter glow in world's above.

### 'WHEN AROUND THEE HOVER THE MAGIC WINGS...'

(submitted 31 August, 1847; printed 9 September, 1847)

When around thee hover the magic wings
Of Hope, and its bright imaginings,
And fancied bliss to thee portray
But to be blasted in a day;

When the fondest objects of thy heart,
Are torn by stern decree apart;
And Friendship, fickle as the wind,
Departs, nor leaves a joy behind!
When stern-eyed Death doth seek its prey;
And sland'rous tongue is heard to say,
Thou art dishonest, proud or vile;
And fortune from thee turns its smile,
If "Life's a jest" there's hope in Hell,
And Death itself is but a spell,
For wearied nature to repose,
And leave behind earth's hourly woes.
A jest indeed! would to God it were;
'T would free us from all present care,
To gain the realms of lasting bliss;
And from the pains that sadden this.
When doom'd to earth's severest ills,
Methinks that "Life's" a bitter pill.

\*\*\*

# IX

## "JONATHAN"

### FLOURISHED 1849

The identity of the versifier who used the pseudonym "Jonathan" remains unknown[56]. This political versifier wrote "The Children Of The Sun" in a condemning response to Loyalist rioters' reaction to The Rebellion Losses Bill, burning the Parliament House in Montreal on 25 April, 1849. At Guelph, in August of 1849 (printed in the *Guelph & Galt Advertiser*), Jonathan had written a poem entitled "The League." This was part of other political poems written for the *Advertiser* and the *Herald* in this year, and also illustrates the versified battle referred to above in sections V and VI, between the two proprietors of the Guelph newspapers; George Pirie (*Herald*), and John Smith (*Guelph & Galt Advertiser*).

These incendiary Guelph political poems include "Ho, gallant soldiers of the League, see that your arms be bright." (Guelph *Herald*, 10 July, 1849); "Rhymes For The Times, No. 1," which begins: "'Ho, gallant soldiers of the League,' the time has come, at length,..." by Ben Brace (junior)[57] (*Guelph & Galt Advertiser*, 2 August, 1849); "Rhymes For The Times, No. 2," which begins: "'Ho, gallant soldiers of the League,' of every age and station,..." also by Ben Brace (*Guelph & Galt Advertiser*, 9 August, 1849); "Rhymes For The Times, No. 4 - Welcome To The Bruce"[58] by Ben Brace (*Guelph & Galt Advertiser*, 23 August, 1849).

Jonathan also wrote "Welcome To Lord Elgin - Written on occasion of his late visit to Guelph," in October of 1849, and printed in the *Guelph & Galt Advertiser* on 1 November, 1849.

---

[56] This "Jonathan" may be Jonathan Wilkinson (see Appendix A: *Advertiser*), or "Brother Jonathan" referred to by "Diogenes Redivivus" (section XIX), or someone else.

[57] See note in Appendix H.

[58] The Governor General, James Bruce, 8th Earl of Elgin (Lord Elgin).

## THE CHILDREN OF THE SUN

(Printed in the *Guelph & Galt Advertiser* 27 September, 1849)

O these pretty little children, you do ask me who
    they be,
The pretty little family who prattle loyalty. _
Yet seem so full of grief and woe, instead of mirth
    and fun,
O these are called, in modern times, the Children
    of the Sun!

You ask me who their Father was - I'll tell you
    of that same, -
A selfish, grasping despot he, and **COMPACT** was
    his name;
By vile, unrighteous means, 'twas said, he rich
    possession won,
And thus he sought to well enrich his Children
    of the Sun.

But age crept on apace, and sorely was old **COMPACT**
    tried,
And through accusing foes, he sickened, gasped,
    and kicked, and died;
His Children wept most bitterly, to see his course
    was run,
But destitute he did not leave the Children of the
    Sun!

For they were clothed, and fat and fair, and
    riches great had made,
For they had learned, and that right well, their
    nice old Father's trade, -
They grasped at everything worth having - no-
    thing did they shun,
That could be made but to enrich the Children
    of the Sun!

But time and tide works strange events, and so
    it came about,
A bigger family grew up, and turned the lesser
    out;
They roared and raved in bitter spite, and said
    'twas cruel fun
Thus to deprive of power and prog, the Children
    of the Sun!

But the Big Family was sturdy, stout Reforming
    Rads,
And vowed that they would have their rights -
    and right ye were, my lads!
Why should a Little Family in plundered riches
    run,
And th' Big one starved to clothe and feed the
    Children of the Sun?

O then these pretty Children - awful furious grew
    their ire,
And so they burned the Council House at Montreal
    with fire,
And sore abused the country's Chief, in flaming
    bullying tone,
For they have hearts of subtle fire, the Children
    of the Sun.

They tell him that he must be still, and keep
    himself at home,
For if he dares to go abroad, full sad will be his
    doom!
And many then shall sleep their last, and blood
    in torrents run, -
O valiant soldier-cubs ye are, ye Children of the
    Sun!

At last to gain their power again, they formed a
    mighty League, _
They cannot work, poor little dears ! and do not
    like to beg;
And hard, tormenting creditors the proudest of
    them dun,
O give them warmest sympathy, - these Children
    of the Sun!

Pity the sorrows of these poor chums - let drop a
    pitying tear,
Don't tell them that they're served just right -
    nor laugh at them, nor jeer!
For though they've gone astray, they may to
    better things be won,
And treatment kind may yet reform the Children
    of the Sun!

\*\*\*

# X

## 𝕽.𝕭.

The identity of this versifier remains unknown. R.B. may be Robert Boyd (see section XVIII), who also occasionally went by his initials, but the potential link is left for future scholarship. R.B.'s poem "Verses Suggested On Seeing A Caged Sky-Lark In Mr Glendinning's Saloon, Guelph," may refer to John Glendinning, who is noted in an 1844 Guelph Indenture of Bargain and Sale as selling property to David Allan.

## VERSES SUGGESTED
## ON SEEING A CAGED SKY-LARK
## IN MR GLENDINNING'S SALOON, GUELPH
("Guelph, 21st May, 1853" Printed in the Guelph *Advertiser* 21 June, 1853)

> I'm not at home in this sorry jail,
> O let me out to soar on high,
> Away with the balmy breeze to sail,
> Filling the air with melody.

> O let me out to dwell with the flowers,
> And sleep by their side through the night;
> Rising at morn 'midst dewy showers,
> Away up to the gates of light.

> Flutt'ring the fleecy clouds among,
> Beyond the reach of human eye; -
> Singing o'er a grateful song,
> To him who made the earth and sky;

To bid your birds their voices raise
    For all the joys the seasons bring;
If ignorant of songs of praise
    I will teach them how to sing.

O let me out your woods to see,
    Where the wild deer at freedom roam;
The boasted land of liberty,
    The exile's dear and happy home.

Then give me freedom, for I was free
    As the breeze that faun'd my speckled breast;
To sing and soar o'er glen and lea,
    In all their summers beauty dress'd.

Soaring high at the early dawn,
    Afar where wild the heather waves,
Singing ofttimes unheard by man,
    A requiem o'er the martyrs' graves.

Then to my secret home would fly
    Among the grass with dew-drops pearl'd;
For though my song is in the sky
    My home is lowly in the world.

Such was my life in Scotia's Isle,
    Where I again would like to be;
I'm alone at home in this prison vile;
    O that I again were free !

\*\*\*

# XI

## 𝔍ohn 𝔓earson

### FLOURISHED 1853 - 1854

John Pearson's life and career remain a mystery. He wrote a poem entitled "A Soliloquy on the Death of a Wife" from Guelph, which was printed in the *Advertiser* on 15 September, 1853. It is also likely he who wrote (signing simply as "J.P") "Lines written on the banks of Lake Huron, for the 'Guelph Advertiser,' by a disconsolate husband upon the premature death of his beloved wife," which was printed in that paper on 20 October, 1853. Pearson's most interesting poem is the following:

## REFLECTIONS ON THE RIVER SPEED, ETC.

("Guelph, 1854" Printed in the Guelph *Advertiser* 28 September, 1854)

> Romantic Speed! unnumber'd rills discharge
> Their liquid treasure in thy crystal stream,
> Which onward flows, impell'd by nature's law,
> Through rugged swamp, and woodland dense and wild, -
> Calm, but restless as the ocean wave.
>
> No scenes majestic mark thy onward course,
> (Like thine, Niagara, of world-spread fame,)
> And nought is heard, but nature's artless voice,
> In perfect harmony with social bliss.
>
> The tow'ring cedar, and the massy pine,
> Extend their branches o'er thy sylvan stream -
> Forming an avenue devoid of art
> Which cultur'd taste might feelingly admire.

Oft has the Angler troll'd his luring bait
Beneath thy canopy's umbrageous shade,
Where speck'led Trout - the sportsman's welcome prize -
Intensely watch to seize the giddy fly,
Which, oft descending, meets a living grave.

No prowling menial, like a famish'd Wolf,
No Tyrant's satellite, a nation's bane,
Can here, insulting, claim exclusive right
To the free tenants of the field and flood.

Rude are thy banks, where vegetable strife
In dense confusion skirt thy ancient bed,
And lave their branches in their lambient wave.

There too, and in the distance scatter'd wide,
Shrouded in moss, and mould'ring in decay,
The aged tenants of the forest sleep;
Which once erect, and cloth'd with vernal grace,
Did brave the fury of a thousand storms.
For death's a paradox - since thence proceed
The vital agencies of plastic life,
Which re-absorb'd, sustain their late compeers,
In all the majesty of woodland pride.
A complex system, perfect in design,
And harmonizing with that endless chain
Of causes multiform, effects benign,
By which pure beneficence design'd to bless
All sentient being, animated dust,
Endow'd with instinct's blind impulsive pow'r,
Or, God-like, reason's nob'ler gift to Man.

But soon the dread, destructive, murd'ring Axe,
Will bare thy bosom to the sun's bright ray,
For ages hid in solitary gloom;
Near which the Red-man pitch'd his rustic camp,
Drank thy pure stream, nor dreamt of liquid fire, -
That awful scourge of their diminish'd race.

'Tis man's prerogative, by heav'n consign'd,
The Earth to cultivate, and to subdue
All noxious being hostile to his weal;
(Creation's lord, amenable, yet free.)
But the poor Indian, dark as nature's night, -
Like the rude diamond, e're the artist's skill
Displays its power of action on the mind, -
Is yet a brother, equal in descent,
With claims to justice, liberty, and life -
Man's birthright, seal'd and register'd in heav'n.
Oppress him not - a righteous judge presides,
Who with judicial punishment inflicts
Just retribution on that lust for wealth
Which manacles the heart to Mammon's shrine
Averts the moral vision of the soul
From heav'n-born virtue' never fading charms
The hallow'd parent of all just design.

Witness, ye blood-stain'd annals of the dead,
Ye murder'd millions 'neath a southern sky,
Despite of regal edicts to restrain
The rabid influence of sordid gain: -
Revolting scene! where Mercy acts no part! -
The savage brute which roams the desert wild,
Abhor'd for cruelty and gory deeds,
(With nought but selfish instinct for his guide)
Is spotless purity, compar'd with man,
Whose sordid soul can seal its guilt with blood.
But Spanish cruelty and haughty pride, -
The sure precursors of a nation's fall, -
Have lick'd the dust - degraded, and despis'd,
In prostrate poverty, and shameless guilt
She wanes through weakness, void of moral strength,
Beneath the judgements of offended heav'n.

\*\*\*

# XII

## 𝕮HARLES 𝕿. 𝕯ANIEL

### FLOURISHED 1864

Sometimes referred to as C.T. Daniels,[59] Charles T. Daniel wrote *William and Annie: or, A Tale of Love and War and Other Poems*, which he printed at Guelph in 1864 at the "Herald" Book and Job Establishment.[60] He dedicated the book "To the fallen heroes of my beloved country this book is respectfully and reverently dedicated by the author." The Introduction provides some interesting historical background to his activities. He was a Rebel soldier during the American Civil War, under the command of John Hunt Morgan (1825-1864), from 4 October 1862 to 19 July 1863. In a campaign intended to divert Union troops and resources in tandem with the twin Confederate operations of Vicksburg and Gettysburg in the summer of 1863, Morgan set off on what was to become known as "Morgan's Raid." Following several skirmishes, the raid almost ended on 19 July, 1863, at Buffington Island, Ohio, when approximately 700 of his men, including Daniel, were captured while attempting to cross the Ohio River into West Virginia. This was also known as the St. Georges Creek Skirmish. Most of Morgan's men captured that day spent the rest of the war in the infamous Camp Douglas Prisoner of War camp in Chicago. On 26 July, near Salineville, Ohio, Morgan and his remaining soldiers were finally forced to surrender. In early November, Daniel escaped from the 'Federal prison' and crossed north into Canada. Some time between November 1863 and May 1864, Daniel resided in Guelph, and appears also to have been familiar with Garafraxa. The further movements and life of this fascinating character, following the publication of his poetry in Guelph, remain for future research.

The note under his poem "The Girls of Guelph" reads "'This song was written after the introduction was in press."[61] We know that on 17 May, 1864,[62] Daniel had his poetry book at the press, and therefore "The Girls of Guelph" was written and/or included into

---

[59] Golick 2010

[60] See Appendix C.

[61] Daniel 1864:Introduction.

[62] Golick 2010: Table 7, page 255.

the volume sometime shortly after that date, and before the book was completed the same year.

## THE GIRLS OF GUELPH

(Published in Guelph, 1864)[63]

When I begin to sing this song,
    'Tis not to please myself;
But just to yield the homage due
    The lovely girls of Guelph.
When I behold their glossy hair
    Done up in nets or curled,
Then I am tempted to declare
    The loveliest in the world.

Chorus.
And when I see their jaunty caps,
    Their dresses neat and gay,
I have to hide my eyes for fear
    They'll steal my heart away.

I love to note their lively talk,
    To hear their cheerful voice,
And there is something in their walk
    To make the ear rejoice.
For there is music in the fall
    Of lightly stepping feet,
As, lithe and joyous, large or small
    Go tripping down the street.

Chorus.
But when I see their jaunty caps,
    Their dresses neat and gay,
I have to hide my eyes for fear
    They'll steal my heart away.

---

[63] Daniel 1864:81-82

Then let the world go as it will,
The wise will happy be,
And I of bliss will drink my fill,
As long as it is free.
So whilst I'm stopping in the town
I will not seek for pelf;
But that I may not win a frown
From any girl in Guelph.

Chorus,
For when I see their jaunty caps, &c.


**WORKS:**

Charles T. Daniel 1864. *William and Annie: or, A Tale of Love and War and Other Poems*. Guelph: "Herald" Book and Job Establishment.

Poems in this book:
"William and Annie - A Tale of Love and War": "The Song of Morgan's Legion"; "The Soldier's Farewell"; "The Lullaby."
"Fugitive Poems" - "My Destiny"; "Leila Runell, A Song"; "A Temperance Song"; "To R *****"; "The Sophomore's Soliloquy"; "An Incident"; "Genius and Plodder"; "Farewell"; "The House Where I Was Born"; "To Jennie"; "The Shamrock. An Irish Song." (Air - "The Soldier's Dream"); "The Girls of Guelph"; "Love and Friendship"; "Lines written on the death of a child struck by lightning"; "The Warning"; "Do I Not Love Thee?"; "The Challenge"; "To The Infidel"; "Epitaphs"; "My Dream"; "Disappointment"; "Lines written on the likeness of a beautiful young lady"; "An Acrostic" [LIZZIE]; "To Mattie; Nelly. A Song"; "To Agnes"; "Goodnight"; "Love"; "The Witling"; "To Anna. A Sonnet"; "The Girls of Garafraxa. A Song" (Air - "The Girl I left behind me"); "To ****"; "To Lilah"; "Second Love"; "A Picture"; "A Song" ("supposed to be sung by a Mexican port on the event of the American invasion"); "A Motto"; "The Tear."

\*\*\*

# XIII

## 𝔥etty 𝔥azelwood

### Flourished 1867-1871

Four poems by Henrietta (Hetty) Hazelwood appeared in the *Guelph Daily Mercury* newspaper from 1867 to 1869. Each, with minor changes, appeared later in her 1871 published book of poetry *A Garland Gathered at Morn. A Collection of Short Poems* (Toronto: Hunter, Rose & Co.). This demonstrates that she was allowing the Guelph newspaper readership to have a first glance of her work. Hazelwood dedicated her book to the memory of Mary Anne McDonald. Two poems, entitled "To Marie Ann"[64] and "Marie Anne,"[65] presumably refer to this person, but the identities of Marie Ann(e) and Hazelwood is left for future research.

### Sleep On

("Written for The Guelph Mercury" Printed 26 October, 1867)[66]

Sleep on, oh young and beautiful; thy bed
Is where the elms their drooping branches wave;
Where sweetest flowers bloom o'er thy buried head,
And chase the shadows from thy woodland grave.

Sleep on, oh young and beautiful; for one
O'er thy long rest a lonely vigil keeps;
And when the stars their midnight watch have sung,
He o'er thy dreamless slumber wakes and weeps.

---

[64] Hazelwood 1871:18-19

[65] Hazelwood 1871:36-37

[66] Also in Hazelwood 1871:42

Sleep on, oh young and beautiful, sleep on,
No more thou'lt waken in this vale of tears;
Thy spirit with the crowned and blood-washed throng,
The roll of life's eternal river hears.

## MOURN NOT THE AGED
('For the Guelph Mercury' printed 9 November, 1867)[67]

Weep when the infant promising and bright,
And clothed in Beauty's softest robes of light,
Tires of the path its infant feet have trod,
And finds the[68] way to heaven and to God.

Mourn when the violet beautiful and sweet
Is crushed to earth by careless, hurrying feet,
And in the dust obscurely, meekly lies,
Emitting gentle fragrance as it dies.

But mourn not when the aged pilgrims go
Forth from these scenes of sorrow and of woe;
Rejoice that their freed spirits to the skies
On wings of Love and Faith[69] may gently rise.

Their work is done, why should they longer stay,
Their souls are longing for the far away;
Their hearts are weary and their feet are sore,
O mourn not that they will return no more.

The flowerets all must droop to earth and die,
The withered leaves upon the ground must lie;
Rejoice that their worn bodies too may rest,
Their spirits find a home among the blest.

---

[67] Also in Hazelwood 1871:22-23

[68] Hazelwood (1871) has changed "the" to "its"

[69] Hazelwood (1871) has changed "Faith" to "peace"

## OVER THE RIVER

("Written for the Mercury" Printed 14 December, 1867)[70]

Over the river I loved to gaze,
    In the years that have gone by,
When the autumn sun's soft lingering rays
    Painted the evening sky.

For it was there that my loved ones of earth
    Dwelt in their happiness free,
And often the sounds of their innocent mirth
    Were borne o'er the waters to me.

But years have sped[71] over me, and left in their track[72]
    But sadness, and sorrow, and care;
They have borne in their course what time cannot bring back,
    For the light of their home is not there.

And now over the river I love to gaze,
    The river so dark and chill,
Where lingers none of the summer[73] haze,
    But the waters are deep and still.

For their voices I hear on the other side,
    In anthems of rapture that flow
Out o'er[74] the waves of the death-cold tide,
    To comfort me here in my woe.

---

[70] Also in Hazelwood 1871:45-46

[71] Hazelwood (1871) has changed "sped" to "passed"

[72] Hazelwood (1871) has changed "track" to "flight"

[73] Hazelwood (1871) has changed "summer" to "autumn"

[74] Hazelwood (1871) has changed "Out o'er" to "Over"

And away on the shore a glory gleams,
    Lighting up river and tree,
From the throne of God that radiance streams,
    'Tis the light of their homes[75] I see.

## LET ME REST

("for the Mercury" Printed 16 May, 1868)[76]

    Sister I am lone, unblest,
      On your bosom let me rest.
Softly fades[77] the evening's light;
I am alone[78] and sad to-night.
Faintly on my spirit flow
Memories of long ago,
Visions of the vanished years
Childhood's hopes, and girlhood's fears,
Dreams of joy that long have fled,
Hopes that withered, and are dead,
Idols that I treasured up,
Longings[79] after fame's bright cup,
Bliss I thought would last for aye,
Pleasures that have passed away.

    I am weary, lone, unblest,
      On your bosom let me rest,
For my idols, one by one,
Have been broken; all are gone,
Dreams too bright for earth to claim,
Dreams of love, and dreams of fame;
And in twilight's deepening gloom
I am weeping o'er their tomb,

---

[75] Hazelwood (1871) has changed "homes" to "home"

[76] Also in Hazelwood 1871:30-31

[77] Hazelwood (1871) has changed "Softly fades" to "Softly falls"

[78] Hazelwood (1871) has changed "alone" to "lone"

[79] Hazelwood (1871) has changed "Longings" to "Yearnings"

Only longing now to lie
Where the low winds gently sigh,
Where the dewy flowers may weep
Softly o'er my dreamless sleep,
Longing for my name to be
Forgotten now by all but thee.
    I am weary, lone, unblest,
    On your bosom let me rest.


## ON THE DEATH OF AN INFANT

("'written for the Guelph Mercury'" Printed 18 January, 1868)[80]

O Hattie, in thy childhood gay,
    Ere thy young feet had learned to roam,
Or from the paths of truth to stray,
    Thy Saviour[81] took thee safely home.

Whilst thou wast[82] with us here on earth,
    We feared thy stay would not be long;
Thy beauty was of heavenly birth
    Thy voice was like the angels' song.

And often to thy visions free
    Came voices from their happy band -
So thin the veil that had hid from thee
    The glories of the better land.

And though we mourn that from our sight
    Thy sunny smile is hid for aye,
And that those eyes of heavenly light
    No more will open on our day;

---

[80] Also in Hazelwood 1871:29-30

[81] Hazelwood (1871) has changed "Thy Saviour" to "The angels"

[82] Hazelwood (1871) has changed "Whilst thou wast" to "When thou was't"

O! we rejoice that from the cares
Of all earth's children thou art free,
And that the Tempter's wiles and snares
Shall[83] have no power over thee,

That with thy sister thou hast found
The land whose glories are untold,
Whose happy children are crowned,
And walk on streets of shining gold,

Whose harp-strings echo sweeter notes
Than mortal ears have ever heard -
Wild music that triumphant floats
O'er seas of crystal softly stirred.

Where silver streamlets gently flow
Through valleys of eternal bloom;
Where fadeless roses brightly grow
And fill the air with rich perfume.

Where cruel death can never stray,
Where there are known no broken ties,
And[84] God himself shall wipe away
The tears from all his people's eyes.

O, may we when earth's storms are o'er,
And life's rough billows cease to play,
Meet those we love to part no more
Through one eternal, blissful day.

---

[83] Hazelwood (1871) has changed "Shall" to "Can"

[84] Hazelwood (1871) has changed "And" to "But"

## OLD YEAR, A KIND GOOD-NIGHT

("Written for the Mercury" Printed in the Evening Mercury 31 December, 1868)[85]

Old Year, a kind good-night,
    Your reign is almost o'er,
Soon we'll see your face no more
    And it makes us very sad to part from you.[86]
Old friend, both true and tried,
    We have journey'd side by side
In your beauty and your pride,
    And your gifts to us were neither mean nor few.
All the hours of joy you cast
    O'er our lives, will soon be past,[87]
Far too bright were they to last,
    But the friends you gave to us are kind and true,
And for this we hold you dear,
    Love your very name, Old Year,
Mourn our parting is so near
    And the hours you have to live have grown so few.
So Old Year, a kind good-night,
    Your reign is almost o'er,
Soon we'll see your face no more,
    And it makes us very sad to part from you.
But we long to see the Right
    Going hand in hand with Light,[88]
And triumphant in the fight,
    Over darkness and oppression in the New.

---

[85] Hazelwood 1871:8-9

[86] Hazelwood (1871) has changed "from" to "with"

[87] Hazelwood (1871) has changed "o'er" to "round"

[88] Hazelwood (1871) has changed these lines to "But we long to see the light - Going hand in hand with right..."

## FLOATING OUT

(printed in the *Guelph Evening Mercury* 15 May, 1869)[89]

Floating out in the twilight gray,
At the beck of a shadowy hand,
From this cold and desolate land
To the beautiful country far away;
Past the loving words and the tender tears,
Past the love of a life and the hope of years.

Floating out in the twilight gray,
And the awful shadow is o'er her now,
But a glory encircles her snowy brow
From the beautiful country far away;
And her bright earth life will shortly seem
Like the memory faint of a troubled dream.

Forty years have passed away
Since she floated out in the twilight gray,
And I wait for the rising of death's cold tide
To bear me away to my angel bride[90];
In the midst of a bright, perpetual day,
In the beautiful country far away.

---

[89] Also in Hazelwood 1871:27

[90] Hazelwood (1871) has changed "...to my angel bride" to "...to my long lost bride"

## The Poet at his Sister's Grave

("written for the Mercury" Printed 17 July, 1869)[91]

Thine was the smile that cheered my pathway dreary,
    And gave me strength when hope forsook my heart;
Thine was the voice that bade me not be weary,
    But in the world's great work to do my part;
That spoke of others, striving[92] and repining,
    Who reaped a harvest in the roll of years -
Thine was the faith that saw the future shining
    Beyond the mists of darkness and of tears.

And now I stand amidst the august splendor,
    Surrounded by my sheaves of golden grain,
And vainly listen for the voice so tender,
    In the sweet praise I ne'er shall hear again;
I stand alone, success has made me brave,
    But what is life to me, and what is fame;
Oh! could[93] I hang my laurels on thy grave,
    And sleep beside thee there without a name.

**Works:**

Hetty Hazelwood 1871. *A Garland Gathered at Morn*. Toronto: Rose & Hunter.

*　*　*

---

[91] Also in Hazelwood 1871:56

[92] Hazelwood (1871) has changed "striving" to "toiling"

[93] Hazelwood (1871) has changed "Oh! could I..." to "Would I could..."

# XIV

## 𝔇avid 𝔐orrison

### Flourished 1869

David Morrison is known for one poem written for the *Guelph Daily Mercury* in 1869. Morrison's name appears at the end of the poem, with the address "Moffat, by Airdrie." Airdrie is a town in North Lanarkshire, Scotland, 19 km east of Glasgow. Ward 11 of Airdrie is Moffat Mills. If, as is implied, David Morrison wrote the poem while at Moffat, it is unknown why he was writing the piece for the *Mercury* in Guelph.

### THE BANKS OF THE CALDER
("written for the Mercury" Printed 26 June, 1869)

Aft, aft hae I lain on the banks of the Calder[94],
    And sang to my Mary, the pride of the lea;
But I'm far frae the banks o' the clear winding Calder,
    I'm far frae my Mary, and Mary frae me.

Cruel misfortune has forced me to wander,
    And seek an asylum in lands o'er the sea;
I sigh to revisit old Scotland's wild grandeur,
    I'm far frae my Mary, and Mary frae me.

Oh, had I the wings o' the swift-flying swallow,
    Soon, soon would I kneel on the land that is free;
I'm here among strangers and manifold dangers,
    I'm far frae my Mary, and Mary frae me.

---

[94] The River Calder may refer to a major tributary of the River Spey in the Highlands, or to a river in Renfrewshire, near Lochwinnoch.

The green-crested lapwing still screams o'er the mountains,
　　Where the bonnie bell-heather blooms lovely to see;
In my slumbering I dream o' Scotland's clear fountains,
　　I'm far frae my Mary, and Mary frae me.

The bagpipe is played in the land o' my fathers.
　　And "Lang Syne" is sung with heart-soothing glee;
But a cloud o' despondence within my heart gathers,
　　I'm far frae my Mary, and Mary frae me.

Her face is as fair as the rose in full blossom.
　　She's harmless as ony[95] wee lamb on the lea;
May hope's golden star shine bright in her bosom,
　　I yet may see Mary, and Mary see me.

Aft, aft hae I lain on the banks of the Calder,
　　And sang to my Mary, the pride o' the lea;
But I'm far frae the banks o' the clear, winding Calder,
　　I'm far frae my Mary, and Mary frae me.

\* \* \*

---

[95] Probably a typographical error for "any"

# XV

## 𝔄LEXANDER 𝔚. 𝔅LYTH

### FLOURISHED 1870

Alexander W. Blyth was born in Glasgow, Scotland, in 1807. He came to the Scotch Block of Guelph Township, on the Elora Road, in 1833 and opened the first hotel in that part of Guelph.[96] For many years he remained an Innkeeper.[97] Blyth wrote the poem "Alma Heights" in 1870, based on the Battle of the River Alma, which took place on 20 September, 1854, during the Crimean War. The victory of Lord Raglan (Britain) and Jacques St. Arnaud (France) over the Russian army is also commemorated in the Guelph street names: Crimea Street; St. Arnaud Street; Raglan Street, Lucan[98] and Alma Street. Similarly, Guelph's Sultan and Omar Streets are named after Mihajlo Latas (better known as Omar Pasha), an Ottoman commander in the Crimean War who defeated Russia at Sevastopol. These streets were all developed during the Crimea War, in 1855 by Sheriff George J. Grange.[99]

The poem is now difficult to find and we are solely reliant upon Johnson's[100] quotation of only "a few stanzas"[101]:

### ALMA HEIGHTS

Here's a health to the land that has sent her sons forth,
To fight for Old England's rights;
From hill, dale and glen came the men of the North,
And their tartans first crowned Alma heights.
Accustomed to roam Scotia's mountains at large,

---

[96] Johnson 1977:336. See Further Reading.

[97] 1871 Canada Census: Ancestry.ca

[98] George Bingham, 3rd Earl of Lucan, who, during the Crimean War, issued the fateful order during the Battle of Balaclava, in October 1854, which led to the tragedy of the Charge of the Light Brigade.

[99] Irwin 1998. See Further Reading.

[100] Johnson 1977

[101] Johnson 1977:336

They ascended the heights like the deer;
Then with shouther to shouther[102] they form'd to the charge,
Then dash'd on with a true British cheer.

*Chorus.*
Then here's to the bonnet, the plume and the hose,
To the sporan, the kilt and the plaid;
To the jacket so smart, and the broad buckled shoes;
Make the garb of the true highland lad.

Here's a health to the land that claims Sir Colin the bold[103],
Stern and rugged her clifts they may be;
But of sterner stuff and ruggeder mold,
Are her sons with the kilt to the knee.
Then intrenchments and batteries, last the redoubts,
Each were carried and won with a cheer;
When Sir Colin look'd round, and the old Lion's shouts
Lads there's nane but our ain highland bonnets seen here...

*Chorus* - Then here's to, etc.

\*\*\*

---

[102] The meaning is "shoulder to shoulder," but we are dependent upon Johnson's transcription, which has this odd spelling.

[103] "Colin the Bold" refers to Sir Colin Campbell, who led three battalions at the Battle of Alma: the 93rd (Highland) Regiment, the 79th (Cameron Highlanders) Regiment and the 42nd (Royal Highland) Regiment.

# XVI

## 𝔍. 𝔓. 𝔅.

**FLOURISHED 1870**

The identity and career of J.P.B. remains unknown.

### TO SEE THEE ONCE AGAIN
("Written for the Mercury" Printed 21 July, 1870)

Were all the streams that sweep along
　　To join the swelling main
But mine to give, I'd give them all
　　To see thee once again.

Were all the trees that stately stand,
　　In sunshine and in rain,
But mine to give, I'd give them all
　　To see thee once again.

Were all earth's hidden hoards of gold,
　　For which men toil in vain,
But mine to give, I'd give them all
　　To see thee once again.

The treasures that beneath the sea
　　For centuries have lain,
Were they but mine, I'd give them all
　　To see thee once again.

The worlds that gem the vaults of night,
 And all these worlds contain,
Were they but mine, I'd give their light
 To see thee once again.

But vain the wish, and vain the thought
 Yes, both alike are vain;
And yet, perchance, 'twill be my lot
 To see thee once again.

For when my weary life is oe'r,[104]
 And free from sin and pain,
I reach at length the shining shore,
 I'll see thee once again.

Yes, when I reach that land of light,
 And view that heavenly train,
With crown of gold and robes of white,
 I'll see thee once again.

\*\*\*

---

[104] Printing error for "o'er" (over).

# XVII

## 𝔍OHN 𝔍NGLIS

### 23 MAY, 1839, HAWICK, SCOTLAND -
### 26 DECEMBER, 1928, HAWICK, SCOTLAND
### RESIDED IN GUELPH 1872 - 1874

John Inglis was by trade a weaver from Hawick, Roxburghshire, Scotland. In 1872 he came to Guelph with his young family and worked at McCrae & Armstrong's hosiery and woollen manufactory at the corner of Huskisson (now Lower Wyndham) and Surrey streets. John Armstrong was also from Hawick, and had been the Baillie there before emigrating to Guelph. In 1878, the Provost of Hawick, Mr. Robert Ewan, visited Guelph, and was met by Armstrong and several other Hawick emigres.[105]

Inglis is not to be confused with another, apparently unrelated, John Inglis, a local Guelph manufacturer.[106] Likewise, he is not another poet named John Inglis (b.1813, Hearthstone, Tweedsmuir).[107] Nor does there appear to be any ancestral connection between the weaver poet and Sir Hugh Inglis, who assisted Guelph pioneer Charles Julius Mickle (see Appendix E) with his appointment as an Extra Clerk with the East India Company in 1803.[108]

The poetic abilities of John Inglis may have been encouraged by David McCrae, partner to Andrew Armstrong of McCrae & Armstrong, father of Lt. Col. John McCrae, and Vice-President of the St. Andrew's Society of Guelph.

Shortly after arriving in Guelph, John and Helen's (*née* Rodger) youngest daughter Bessie Scott Inglis died 2 September, 1872.[109] Following this tragedy, John wrote "Bessie's

---

[105] Articles on the Provost of Hawick visiting Guelph are in the *Daily Mercury*; 15 July, 1878 and 12 October, 1878, in which Ewan relates a challenge between the Guelph and Hawick curling clubs.

[106] John Inglis, the Guelph manufacturer, was born in 1828 in the parish of Castleton, Roxboroughshire, Scotland (Johnson 1977:259-260). This John Inglis ran a foundry in Guelph under the company name Inglis & Hunter.

[107] John Inglis 1866. "Poems and songs." Printed for the author by Ballantyne, Roberts, & Co. Edinburgh. This John Inglis is mentioned in 1883 by Edwards, in volume 5 of his *Modern Scottish* Poets, who published, in 1866, "Poems and songs," writing the preface February 5th from his residence at 10 Leven Street, Edinburgh.

[108] Crowley 1987:9

[109] Bessie Scott Inglis, daughter of John & Helen, was born 9 May, 1871 and died 2 September, 1872, in Guelph, aged 18 months. Apparently, she was buried at Meaford, Ontario. John Inglis (1907:88-89) wrote "Bessie's Grave" in response to this tragedy.

Grave." By 1874, John Inglis and his family lived at #6 Gordon Street,[110] Guelph, but the grieving family decided, in that year, to returned to Hawick, Scotland. Despite the short time spent in Guelph, it is now certain that at least the poem "Fancy" and perhaps "To Canada," "The Borderer Abroad" and "Borderland" may each have been composed here.

For over twenty years John Inglis was the Curator of Hawick Museum, and the author of a book of verse *Borderland and other Poems*, besides several local songs, the best-known being "Hawick Among the Hills."[111] Inglis died suddenly on Boxing Day of 1928, in his 90th year, at Hawick, and is buried there in Wellogate Cemetery. He was "the last surviving member of the Border Bards Association, formed in February, 1878."[112] Interest in his poetry remains strong. Through the liaising assistance of Zilla Oddy (Hawick Heritage Hub), the living descendants of John Inglis have been extra-ordinary in sharing their family information with me. They were, until now, unaware of the poet's Canadian location.

Edwards (1881)[113] wrote of John Inglis:

> He was trained to the frame-work knitting, at which he continued for twelve years, when he went into one of the tweed factories. In 1872 he removed to America,[114] where he succeeded well, but his heart was so strongly attached to the wild and historic scenery of his much-loved Teviotdale, that he returned home in 1874. In 1879 he published a volume entitled "Borderland." The work was a success, and it is but right to mention that the poet handed over the profits as a gift to the building fund of St John's Church, Hawick, then in course of erection. He sings with much force and vigour the praises of his native vale.[115]

In 1879, Inglis published in Scotland his *Borderland and other Poems* (Kelso), but, four years prior, in 1875, his poem "Borderland" was printed in the *Guelph Daily Mercury*. This was subsequently reprinted on the front page of the same newspaper on Saturday, 31 January, 1914:

---

[110] 1874 Assessment Rolls, Guelph; South Ward (page 37). The 1873 Guelph Directory notes: 'Inglis, John, weaver, r[esidence] Surry [Surrey Street].

[111] *Transactions of the Hawick Archaeological Society*. 1966. Hawick Archaeological Society. Scott & Paterson, Limited. Page 31. Inglis' poem "Hawick Among the Hills" was cited in the 1863 Transactions of the Hawick Archaeological Society; page 86.

[112] *The Hawick Express and Advertiser*; 28 December, 1928.

[113] David Herschell Edwards 1881. *One Hundred Modern Scottish Poets: With Biographical and Critical Notices*. Brechin: D.H. Edwards. Pp. 236-237.

[114] Even these early biographical notes fail to mention Guelph as his place of destination or residence, "America" being a rather misleading gloss.

[115] Edwards 1881:236

The Following stirring poem was printed in the Guelph Mercury, of 1875, together with the following explanatory note: - Borderland. The following beautiful poem was written by John Inglis, formerly a weaver in Armstrong & McCrae's factory, in this Town, and will be read with interest by his many friends here.

It is interesting that John Thomson, in his 1879 introduction to Inglis' poetry book, made the following observation:

> Gay[116] speaks of poets as a peculiar class, 'who live on fancy and feed on air.'[117]

One can only guess if James Gay[118] read this.

The 1879 published version of Inglis' poem "Borderland" has several differences to the earlier version printed in the 1875 *Mercury*.[119] These differences are footnoted below at the appropriate parts of the poem, and demonstrate that Inglis allowed the Guelph public to first read his original draft.

## BORDERLAND

(Reprinted in the *Guelph Daily Mercury* on Saturday January 31st, 1914;
originally printed in the same paper in 1875[120])

They tell of merry England - its
palaces and halls
Which tower above its leafy woods,
their old embattled walls;
But, oh, give me the shielings[121] where
the heath and thistles wave
O'er the rugged hero's cairn and the
gentle martyr's grave!
There playful zephyrs lightly waft
fresh fragrance from the fell,

---

[116] John Gay, author of *The Beggar's Opera* (1728).

[117] Inglis 1879:v

[118] see section XXVII.

[119] As supposed from the surviving 1914 *Mercury* reprint.

[120] The 1875 *Daily Mercury* archives do not fully survive. Thankfully, this poem was reprinted in 1914.

[121] Shielings (sheiling/sheeling/shealing) is Scottish Gaelic for a collection of huts and also a mountain pasture used for grazing cattle in summer. Inglis appears to be using the word in the latter sense.

And Inverocks[122] 'mid the fleecy cloud
    their lays triumphant swell,
To charm the Scottish maidens, till in
    song their voices blend
Round the cosy cottage homes of the
    bonnie Borderland.[123]

When Winter, in his hoary robe,
    haunts mountain sides and groves,
And Boreas[124], with an angry howl,
    through naked woodlands roves,
There's joy within the shieling of the
    blithesome Border wight[125],
By his bonnie blazing fire, when day-
    light dies in night.
As he leans back in his settle, he gazes
    with delight
To the joist where hangs the claymore[126]
    with basket hilt[127] so bright,
That was wielded by his sires, who
    died but would not bend
To sacrifice the freedom of the bonnie
    Borderland.

In fields where noble Wallace[128] led they
    bravely bore the brunt,
When fortune's tide seemed ebbing,
    they still kept form and front,
Till fell the great-souled hero, in the
    noontide of his fame.

---

[122] Inverocks = mountains.

[123] "bonny Borderland" (Edwards 1881:236) / "bonnie Borderland" (*Mercury* 1914).

[124] Boreas: the North wind.

[125] wight: a creature or person.

[126] claymore: Scottish Gaelic for great sword, used from the 15th to 17th centuries.

[127] The basket-hilted sword is contemporaneous with the Claymore great sword.

[128] William Wallace died 23 August, 1305. A Scottish landowner and one of the main leaders during the Wars of Scottish Independence.

And left stern Scotland weeping o'er
    the treachery and shame.
But Bruce's[129] war-cry echoed with ven-
    geance wild and high,
From Carrick's[130] frowning turrets proud
    Edward[131] to defy;
Then rushed the belted yeomen, with
    spear and sweeping brand,
From the cosy cottage homes of the
    bonnie Borderland.[132]

Then wild the cry of battle rose, and
    wide the carnage spread,
While lunged each gleaming weapon,
    and on with death they sped
Shouting loud in triumph[133] as they trod
    the crimson'd plain,
When the flowery earth was sodden
    with the hot blood of the slain,
But still the conflict deepened with
    each continuous shock,
Till England's proudest squadron in[134]
    wild confusion broke;
The fury of the onset no foemen could
    withstand,[135]
When they charged for Bruce and
    freedom, and the bonnie Border-
land.

---

[129] Robert I, "the Bruce" (1274-1329), reigned as King of Scots 1306-1329.

[130] Carrick saw some involvement in the Scottish wars of independence under Robert Bruce, which culminated in his victory over the English at Bannockburn in 1314.

[131] Edward I (1239-1307), King of England 1272-1307.

[132] The end of the third, fifth and final (seventh) stanzas: "cozy cottage homes" (Edwards 1881:237) / "cosy cottage homes" (*Mercury* 1914).

[133] In the 1879 published version this line is: "As they shouted loud in triumph they trod..." (Inglis 1879:4).

[134] "Till old England's proudest..." (Inglis 1879:4).

[135] "Their wild and furious onset no foeman could withstand" (Inglis 1879:4).

In days of persecution, when the[136]
    tramp of armed men
Made them seek the dark seclusion of
    the deep and lonesome glen,
There to suffer cold and hunger without
    one fret or frown,
And at last pour forth their life-blood
    for the martyr's fadeless crown.
Whence came these martyred preachers
    the holy and the brave,
Who suffered in the woodland, the
    moorland, and the cave,
For their worship, pure and simple,
    which no despot e'er could rend[137]
From the cosy cottage homes of the
    bonnie Borderland?

Or whence the bards and minstrels[138]
    who sang in days gone by
The strain that's ever ringing, the[139]
    song that ne'er must die?
They touch the sympathetic chords,[140]
    and noble thoughts impart;
They swell, in cottage and in hall,
    each patriotic heart;
They charm the lonely bushman, in his
    cabin far away;[141]
They nerve the soldier in the van in
    danger's darkest day;
They build a mighty pillar, which[142]

---

[136] "Mid the gloom of persecution,..." (Inglis 1879:4).

[137] "Which despots ne'er could rend" (Inglis 1879:5).

[138] "Whence heroic bards and minstrels" (Inglis 1879:5).

[139] "The noble strain that's ever ringing,..." (Inglis 1879:5).

[140] "They touch the sympathetic chord,..." (Inglis 1879:5).

[141] "They have charms for lonely bushman in cabins far away..." (Inglis 1879:5).

[142] "They have built a mighty pillar,..." (Inglis 1879:6).

Time shall e'en defend,
That it may tell who lived and loved
the bonnie Borderland.

Where joy is ever springing, oh, may
it never cease[143]
To be the hallowed resting-place of
piety and peace!
There at eve the toiling peasant can
read the Word of God,
And teach the children of his care
Salvation's blissful road.
Thus they grow to men and maidens,
in beauty and in might,
With virtue for their guiding star to
tread the world aright
Clinging fast to truth and justice, that
blessings may descend,
On the cosy cottage homes of our
bonnie Borderland.

Hawick                                    John Inglis


## FANCY

(c.1872-4)

One lovely morn when spring had clothed
Ontario's landscape fair,
I turned me to the forest wild,
Away from toil and care;

And as I trod Speed's rugged vale[144],
In pensive mood I gave
Free fancy to the passing gale,
Which bore it o'er the wave-

---

[143] "Where pure joy is ever springing, Oh, never may it cease" (Inglis 1879:6).

[144] The Speed River was named by Guelph founder John Galt in 1827. A major road now called Speedvale crosses the river east-west. Inglis could have been strolling (sometime between 1872 and 1874) along any part of the valley of the Speed from the city of Guelph.

Back to the cottage by the burn,
    Where oft a boy I played,
Exploring every nook and turn,
    And darkling hazel shade

And gathered the yellow cowslips,
    And primrose pale and sweet,
And gowans with the crimson lips
    That bloomed around my feet.

Methought I roamed the dun hillside
    Where Teviot's waters rise,
And heard the laverocks in their pride
    Sing loudly from the skies;

And as I climbed the lofty brow
    Which overlooked the vale,
I learned I ne'er had loved till now
    My native Teviotdale.

I gazed around me and beheld
    The scenes of feud and fray.
And towers which Scott and Douglas held
    In their rough daring day

Against unnumbered foemen, led
    By chiefs of mighty name,
Who fiercely fought and freely bled
    To win heroic fame.

Then, turning to the western fell,
    Where our forefathers trod
Beneath their feet the heather bell
    On their way to worship God,

I saw the hill and pulpit rock
    Where stern old Peden[145] preached
Salvation to his wandering flock,
    So wrongfully impeached.

In joyous mood among these hills
    I sped my airy flight,
By sunny lakes and sighing rills,
    And gliding streamlets bright;

I swept o'er moor and mountain range
    On wings of fancy fleet;
But ere I wist, or dreamt of change,
    Speed rolled beneath my feet.[146]

## WORKS:

"Borderland" - printed in the *Guelph Daily Mercury* in 1875 and 1914. Published in Edinburgh in 1879.

John Inglis 1879. *The Border Land, and Other Poems*. Kelso: J. & J.H. Rutherford.

John Inglis 1907. *Borderland and other Poems*. Hawick: W. & J. Kennedy, Hawick. Printed by Vair & McNairn. A copy of this, once in the ownership of a Mr Thomas Proudfoot of Hawick, now resides in the University of Guelph McLaughlin Library - Archives and Special Collections.

Two John Inglis poems are included in Robert Murray's 1897 edition, *Hawick songs and song writers*. W. & J. Kennedy; "Hawick Among the Hills" (page 60), and "Bonnie Briery Hill" (page 61).

John Inglis and his works are listed in James Stinton's *Bibliography of Works Relating to, or Published in, Hawick*. Hawick: Vair & McNairn, "News" Office,[147] 1908:
Inglis, John, Wilton, Hawick. *The Border Land and other Poems*. 8vo. Kelso, 1879.
Inglis, John, Wilton, Hawick. *Border Land, and other Poems*. Introduction by R.S. Craig, M.A., LL.B. 8vo. Hawick 1907.[148]

* * *

---

[145] The Reverend Alexander Peden (1626-1686), also known as "Prophet Peden", was one of the leading figures in the Covenanter movement in Scotland (Chisholm, Hugh ed. (1911). *Encyclopaedia Britannica* (11th edition). Cambridge University Press).

[146] John Inglis, 1907:90-92

[147] *The Hawick News*, started 26th January, 1882, and published by Messrs Vair & McNairn.

[148] It is this 1907 edition which now resides in the Archives and Special Collections of the University of Guelph McLaughlin Library.

# XVIII

## Robert Boyd

1797, Ayrshire, Scotland -
1880, Guelph, Canada
Resided in Guelph 1830 - 1880

Robert Boyd was "born in Ayrshire, Scotland, 1797; died in Guelph, 1880. He received a liberal education in Scotland and came to the Paisley Block, as a pioneer, in 1830, where he purchased a farm and settled. From an early date he took a prominent part in the affairs of the settlement, and being a writer of some note, his poetic talent was more than once laid under tribute to illustrate the primitive life of those days. While he frequently contributed to the press, as well as occupying the honorary position of Bard of the St. Andrew and Caledonian Societies, he published several creditable books. One of the ablest and best known of his productions in "The Shanty", which is a truthful and humorous picture of those unsophisticated times. He was also successful as a farmer. He married Margaret Inglis, and left one son and one daughter. The latter is now resident of the North West Territories. Mr. Boyd retired to Guelph in 1876, where he died four years later [1880]."[149] In 1851, Robert Boyd was elected a member of the first Town Council of Guelph.[150]

### VERSES ON ST. ANDREW'S DAY
("Written for the Guelph *Mercury*" printed 9 December, 1867)

Auld Scotia, your kinsfolk hear
　　Assembled now in festive ha';
To us you still are fondly dear,
　　Though many a lang, lang mile awa'.

---

[149] *Historical Atlas of the County of Wellington, Ontario.* Toronto: Historical Atlas Publishing Co., 1906.

[150] Burrows 1877:67.

For time nor place can e'er efface
    The filial love we bear to thee;
Nor can we e'er forget the days
    When callants rantin' round your knee.

We're glad to hear you're hale and weel,
    Unscath'd by age, a matron stout,
And routh o' baith gude milk and meal
    To a' your bairnies roun' about

And that you still can act your part
    Amang the honor'd and the great;
Still clear in head and stout in heart,
    And staunch and true to Kirk and State.

'Tis true your hill are far away,
    We canna' see their stalwart forms
Peering amang the cloudlets grey,
    Unmov'd amidst the loudest storms.

Nor does the daisy meet the eye,
    A spotless gem on dewy sod;
Nor can we hear the lark on high
    Warble sweet her hymn to God.

We list not to the burnie's sang,
    As down the glen it wends its way,
Nor hear the deep green woods amang,
    The blackbird pipe his ev'ning lay.

Nor do we see the yellow broom
    Waving on the sunny brae,
Or prickly whins in gowden bloom,
    Where linties sing the live lang day,

Or cairnies grey where heroes fell,
    That you and yours might still be free,
And martyrs' stones, whose records tell
    The death they died for liberty.

Nor can we stand entranc'd to gaze
    On mountain-stream and flow'ry dell,
Made classic by the poet's lays,
    And by the wizard's magic spell.

But still in memory's eye they're near,
    In all their radiance back they come,
And standing out full, fair and clear,
    A transcript of our native home.

Auld Scotia hear this our prayer,
    Lang, lang may ye in wealth be spared,
And may your sons and daughters fair
    Still merit heaven's kind reward.

        R. B. Paisley Block, 5th December, 1867

## THE BACHELOR IN HIS SHANTY
(c.1875)

'Tis somewhat strange a chiel like me
Should frue his native country flee,
And leave his friends o' social glee -
    And loves sae dear.
And cross the braid Atlantic sea
    In quest o' gear.

To come to this strange land o' trees,
This vile abode o' frogs and fleas,
Wi' no ane near to sympathise,
    Or yet to hate us;
Devoured alive by slow degrees
    By curs'd mosquitoes.

To tremble 'neath the ague's power,
Cauld and het, hour after hour,
Drinkin' vile Peruvian stour
    And Ironwood sass,
Wi' mony ither auld wif'e cure -
    Wud kill an ass!

Roasted by the summer's heat -
Till life's weak pulse can scarcely beat,
Half-drown'd in streams o' creeshy sweat
    That gem my beard,
As thick as morning's dewy weet,
    On flow'ry sward![151]

## A FAREWELL TO MY AULD HAME

"The following lines were written by Mr. Robert Boyd on the occasion of his leaving the farm in Paisley Block where he had found a home for nearly fifty years, to take up his residence in Guelph, and were recited by him on the evening of the presentation made him by his friends on the evening of the 4th [Tuesday, 4 April, 1876]."[152]

My lov'd auld hame, adieu, adieu!
    Our parting well may claim a tear
For while my heart to life beats true,
    To me you ever will be dear.

For many years you were to me
    A'the hame in life I had,
However lowly you might be
    You were my ain - and I was glad.

---

[151] Wellington County Museum archive Accession Number A1985.110, archive record 11226. Description: "Slide made by Gordon Couling in March 1978 of the poem, 'The Bachelor in his Shanty,' by Robert Boyd of Guelph Township, ca. 1875; slide made from a newspaper clipping."

[152] *Mercury & Advertiser* newspaper; 7 April, 1876.

For hame's aye hame, 'tis truly said,
    And such you ever proved to me,
In a' my wand'rings far and wide,
    I gladly aye returned to thee.

The poor man's hut is dear to him
    As lordly squire with palace blest,
Though rough his path through life and dim,
    'Tis there he finds a welcome rest.

'Twas there, your lowly roof beneath,
    I welcom'd hame a loving spouse,
She sleeps now in the arms of death,
    In his lone, dark and narrow house.

'Twas there, like music to my ear,
    I heard th' endearing name of father,
And sweeter still, a mother dear,
    Round which our feelings fondly gather.

There round thy fields I've often strayed,
    Kind Nature's wond'rous feats to mark,
An I see the progress she had made
    In her unceasing, changeful work.

To hear the rustling of the corn,
    While waving in the passing breeze,
And songsters sweet at e'en and morn
    Sing o'er their sangs amang the trees,

To muse and loiter by the burn[153]
    That by my cotrins[154] merrily,
Singing blythe at each jouk[155] and turn,
    As on it wimpled to the sea.

---

[153] In Scotland and North East England a "burn" is a name for watercourses from large streams to small rivers.

[154] quatrains: a type of poetic stanza consisting of four lines. Boyd's poem has 16 stanzas with the rhyme scheme ABAB, and AAAA in the tenth stanza.

[155] Scottish for swoop, swerve, jerk.

There oft when Boreas frae the north
      Blew loud and cau'd his biting storms,
Would gather round my humble hearth
      Lov'd women fair, and manly forms,

To talk wi' joy the hale night lang,
      And o'er our troubles crousely craw,
And cheer our hearts wi' some sweet sang
      Of our lov'd Scotland far awa'.

O, these to me are tender ties,
      Will ever in my heart preside,
And Paisley Block a name I'll prize
      'Bove all in our Dominion wide.

And while that light shall glad my eyes,
      And smiling hope my mind illumes,
For lov'd friends there my prayer will rise
      For blessings on their happy homes.

And when on earth their wand'rings cease,
      Their trials done and warfare o'er,
Then may they all arrive in peace
      in Heaven's home to part no more.

And this kind boon from them I seek,
      That I may still remember be,
And try of me to kindly speak
      And a' my many fauts forgie[156].

For we are oft (our conscience warns)
      Driven along on error's tide;
We're ane and a' John Tamson's bairns[157],
      And ever apt to step aside.

---

[156] faults forgive

[157] The popular phrase "We're a' Jock Tamson's Bairns" is Lowland Scots and Northumbrian English for "We're all John Thomson's children." Toronto poet Alexander McLachlan wrote the poem "We're A' John Tamson's Bairns" (McLachlan, Alexander 1861. *The Emigrant: And Other Poems*. Toronto: Rollo & Adam pp.126-128).

**WORKS:**

A collection of handwritten poetry by Robert Boyd, ca. 1850-1878, is in the Wellington County Museum archives: Accession Number A1995.96. The poems are:
"The Address to John Frost;" "A Welcome to the Marquis of Lorne and his Beloved Princess;" "Verses Suggested on Reading the Life of the Scotch Naturalist Edwards;" "A Rhyme for the Times;" "Epistle to Thomas Laidlaw;" "Paisley Block;" "Epitaph on Mr. John Black;" "To Mrs. John Davidson;" "Verses Spoken at the Meeting of the Sons of St. Andrew, 9th December 1878;" "The Scottish Gathering 1st Oct. 1878;" "To Mr. John Anderson On Receiving From Him Two Sprigs of Heather;" "On the Near Approach of Death;" "The Joys of a Loving Home;" "The River St. Lawrence;" "Thoughts Suggested On Visiting the Grave of My Departed Wife;" "Stanzas;" "Verses Suggested on the death of an old friend J. C." [John Cleghorn]; "The Happy Age in Which We Now Live."

\*\*\*

# XIX

## "𝔇IOGENES 𝔕EDIVIVUS"

### FLOURISHED 1875

In the *Town of Guelph Directory* for 1875/6/7 (pages 24-32) appears a scathing satyrical versified lampooning tour of Guelph, written 5 October, 1875, fully transcribed here:

### DIOGENES REDIVIVUS[158].

Traveller - see Guelph and die: -

Not in virtue of spiritual revelations to the olfactory sentient organism from Allan's world renowned Distillery, for our townsman's spirits are high, genial and up to proof, as is easily capable of proof. The whiskey is good. Nothing bad ever left Guelph. - Have we not a vigilant "chief?" Many bad things enter our town but are straightway converted; thanks to the Temperance league who prosecute everything upon two legs, or four, that breaks the law "after hours." To those whose pure perceptions see in whisky nothing but the fetid ichor of Infernus be it known, at any cost, that Allan's whisky is excepted. It gives strength to the weak, courage to the craven, inspires a butcher with poetry[159], sweetens the prosaic grocer's sands of life as benignly as he ever sanded his sugar. Glance with me through yon open doorway.

> "A young voice rises upon the breeze
> Singing a merry nursery rhyme."

"Halt, traveller, or you step upon the bones of a tailor!' There he lies in the plenitude of exultant manhood, blinking up at the table which knew him but knows him not. There he lies, cross-legged, sewing imaginary coats with a threadless needle, singing

"I'm afloat, I'm afloat on the deep rolling sea."

---

[158] Literally "Diogenes Reborn". Diogenes likely refers to Diogenes of Sinope (412-323 BC), the philosopher, better known as "Diogenes the Cynic" or simply "Diogenes".

[159] The identity of this Guelph versifying butcher is uncertain.

"Dear, dear me, wot a spectercle. Lost - lost!"

It is a Temperance leaguer, who having stealthily neared the spot, pauses undecidedly. He recognizes a patient, but for the life of him doesn't know whether to fetch the doctor, the parson, or the "chief."

"I'm afloat, I'm afloat on the deep rolling sea" -

Ugh!-ugh! ua-ua-ue-ui-uo-ua-ah!

Reader, please fill up the blanks yourself, as our tailor did for himself. Reflect, if you list, with me, upon the solemn passage in Ecclesiastes, which, misplaced as it may be, is not inapplicable - "Who knoweth whither goeth the life of the Beast."

"Afloat you are, but where, oh, where will you land?" - queries the Leaguer, with lengthy visage.

"Guess he's landed, friend" - we venture - "on the floor." The Leaguer replies by a solemn head shake, then hurries away. - When he reaches home he will down on his marrowbones to thank the Lord he is not as yon poor sinner!

'Here!-hold!-stop! turn back!' we shout to the retreating figure. -

The Leaguer turns. "Why is Allan's whisky like sin?" "That's no riddle" - responds he moodily - "it *is* sin." "That's begging the question, friend, as you and those of your kidney are apt to do: - because its odour is worse than its taste. Now, go home and stick the champagne labels I see peeping out of your pocket upon the soda-water bottles you ordered last night for the morrow's Temperance banquet.

Now, onward.

This is the Railway Bridge, a notable structure, spanning the valley through which tumbles over dam and race the laughing Speed -

> "I pass thro' ranks of houses stern
> With many a dilly-dally,
> To join the Eramosa branch
> Way yonder in the valley!"

You may stand under the bridge, if you will, your hat drawn over your closed eyes, and listen to the rippling plash of the waters, and dream of woodlands wild, and Indian canoes and tomahawks and catfish, and sniff from afar the exhilarating steams of 'barley-brae' - but keep upon the sidewalk and dodge passing teams, as you love your toes. Hark!

"The ghosts of days departed come thundering down the slopes, clad in pale moonbeams" - no: Ossian never wrote that - crinoline and Grecian bends, deerskin and wampum, breeks[160] and homespun - anything that is poetical.

Softly: it is only the 2:30 express. Stand still, keep your head down and be galvanized gratis. What! a cinder down your back? Never mind; set up for a martyr; it pays now-a-days. This railway bridge is remarkable as being the famous location of trial by ordeal, an institution yet believed in, in Guelph. Parliamentary voters suspected of corrupt practices are caught up by the heels and tied to a plank beneath the bridge, their persons muffled up in blankets, except the nose, which is bare and rubbed with whisky. By and bye comes thundering past the 2:30 express, and he upon whose nose rests a cinder; or which is seen to burn with a lambent blue flame, is known not to be the miscreant. Quite simple, my dear sir; it saves lawyer's fees. The custom seems to explain a certain ruddy appearance peculiar to the nasal extremities of our public men and which slander might easily wrest to its own interpretation.

Here we have the gas-works. A gassy people we. Witness the immense meter, which recently burst, to the great horror of many innocent folks, whose latter end rose awfully into view at the intimation.

"Will she burst, Dick?" - queries an artless urchin of his mate. "Guess not," is the dubious reply.

"If she do, we'll all go up, Dick," pursues the young inquisitor. "Guess *you* won't," is the curt rejoinder. "How - why?" "See any green? Scat, you soft warmint!"

"We are a gassy people - we,
We light our streets so gaily, O.
We are as proud as proud can be
So we scrub our meter daily, O.

(Chorus) O wouldn't I like to meet her, to meet her, to meet her,
O, wouldn't I like to meet her at Victoria Bridge alone!

We light our streets and warm our feets
With gas that costs us dearly, O.
Yet this meter's the first that ever burst
And we pay the piper cheerily, O."

(Chorus)

---

[160] Scottish term for breeches / trousers.

This is the Custom House. From here we send Jews harps, bodkins, and bananas over the lines, which run away along Waterloo Road. Enter, gentlemen. Here are to be found the amenities which supply a lustre to the civilization of the day. It is not in the heart of society that you must look for true courtesy, but upon the border-line where Brother Jonathan and Young Canada shake hands in polished amity to negotiate pork. Enter - be seated: take a ciga-ar. - Of course we have customs of our own. What people of enlightenment have not? Do not our St. Andrews' Society meet once a year at the Queens'[161] to grasp just sufficient of the skirts of sin to remind its members of their humanity? Oh, brother 'I' and brother 'M' - don't you remember? - arm-in-arm, you know, a moonlight night, and a sufficiency of cracks in the sidewalk to make the trail certain and -

"In the wee sm' hours o' the mornin'
We'll a' gang toddlin' hame!"

Of course we have customs! Don't we ennoble our superannuated taverns by converting them into Collegiate Institutes, governed under strictly Temperance auspices?

We teach the young idea how to shoot
On boards where aged vice oft shot the cat.

This delightful ditty contains no malice, gents; it was not aforethought, gents; it came *currente calamo*,[162] gents, like the Pope's Athanasian Pastorals[163].

Still undoubtedly we have customs. -Don't we leave our drains uncovered and dig pitfalls outside our doctors' surgeries, to draw custom for our respectable citizens? But why quarrel with the paternal dispensations of our City Fathers? To do evil that good may come is nothing new. And it is within the range of probabilities that the Town Council may have in their possession some secret receipe (*sic*: recipe) for the Balm of Gilead[164] that is seen put up in green boxes, so neatly, in our flourishing drug stores. Perhaps they get a percentage on the amount sold - *wem geht es an?*[165]

---

[161] The Queens Hotel was on Douglas Street (see note 293, page 148).

[162] *currente calamo*: offhand, without deep reflection.

[163] Pope Pius IX (16 June 1846-7 February 1878). 'Athanasian Pastorals' may be an intentionally garbled reference to the Athanasian Creed (*Quicunque Vult*).

[164] Balsam

[165] *wem geht es an* - German: "To whom does it go?" (translation by Nick Ford).

Besides -

What, tho' we revel in open drains,
Since, they can dodge, who have the brains?

*En avant mon ami!*[166] Before you looms a vast structure, ever being augmented, never to be finished - like the celebrated Cathedral of Cologne in that respect - but whether through a like violation of his compact with the arch-fiend, by the architect[167], is uncertain. You view our Town Hall! Originally, an unassuming building, it has, at irregular intervals, given birth to parasitic excrescences, until, to-day, it resembles a warty toad. Ah, but hath not even the toad a precious jewel in its eye? The front windows of our Hall still dispense light and beauty to the loungers at the doors of the taverns opposite[168]. And now devolves upon the chronicler a duty of supreme pleasure. The fountaius form, ever, a poetical adjunct to the aesthetic display of a city. In connexion with a fountain, one thinks of nightingales, dark-eyed lasses with brown pitchers upon their heads - and such ankles! - mocking-birds and clean linen. Alas; our Town Pump hath no such glories. Sooth, it hath lost its ladle, and looks decrepit and dejected. Of all the feathered songsters, only the mocking-birds remain: the only strains of melody - "Say, Bill, be that a stranger? let's shy half a brick at him!" *Vade retro, Sathanas!*[169]

You stand, now, at the corner of the Bank of Commerce. Your hands clasped behind your back, your extremities grandly diverged to include the sidewalk, you look a veritable collossus (*sic*) of roads (excuse the pun), as you gaze down the majestic length of Wyndham Street. Through the Bank window you see sleek, well-fed, be-oiled and be-starched young men fingering dollar bills so glibly that you wonder they never miss their touch, or that none of these bits of flimsy paper ever stick to their fingers. Taking a few majestic paces forward, you pass an Ossianic Tailor-hero's establishment, then a veritable Horsman,[170] upon the sidewalk, until passing by Chance over the crossing, you meet a Hewer, and a Drawer - of Guelph beer. Away at the other end of the street, bristles a wonderful Boar, a learned Hog, religious, and a ladies' pet. You shortly come upon Heffernan's clothing store, over which Brittannia (*sic*) sits frowning, and ruling the waves, it is to be presumed, of

---

[166] *En avant mon ami* - French: "Forward, my friend" (translation by Nick Ford).

[167] Joseph Connolly was the architect of the present Church of Our Lady Immaculate. Construction began in 1875 and was finally dedicated in 1888.

[168] Namely, the King Edward Hotel.

[169] *Vade retro, Satana*: Latin for "Step back, Satan". This is a Medieval Catholic formula for exorcism, traditionally associated with the Benedictines. Vade retro, Sathanas would mean "Step back, demons".

[170] Horsman, and other names mentioned, were Guelph store owners along Wyndham Street.

pants and overclothes. In her hands is a toasting-fork[171], which so many of her foes have cause to rue. From her position and attitude, the designer evidently meant to post her up as a warning to pretension, so decidedly does she threaten to transfix Dishonesty in high places. This is Rutherford's. But, up aloft, what monstrous growth of preadamite[172] ages is this?

> Be it the great Leviathan
> That once did roam the deep,
> Whom Noah h'isted from the ark
> 'Cos he cost too much to keep?
>
> No, no, it bean't Leviathan,
> Nor don't he cost no keep;
> He's just as harmless and as kind
> As ere a new-killed sheep.
>
> It be the mighty Mastodon
> What lodged in Puslinch Swamp[173],
> He took a Bronkeel trouble onct
> Jest of the frightful damp.
>
> O dear, O dear - to hear him wheeze -
> It shocked the country side:
> It shook the apples from the trees;
> 'Twas lucky that he died.
>
> The crowner[174] sat upon his corpse. -
> They stuffed him up with straw;
> And hung him up agin yon board,
> Where still he laughs - ee - aw!!

*"Ille dolet vere, qui sine teste dolet: requiescat in pace."*[175]

---

[171] Sardonically referring to the trident traditionally held by Britannia.

[172] Before Adam.

[173] Possibly an intriguing reference to a discovery of this prehistoric mammal's bones being discovered in Puslinch Lake some time before 1875.

[174] coroner

[175] "He mourns honestly who mourns without witnesses" (Martial). *Requiescat in pace* = Rest In Peace.

How are your grinders? Rayther abrupt question, I grant, but Dr. Campbell[176] will ask you the same, if you meet him on the street or at the opera - we cultivate the acquaintance of La Traviata occasionally at the Drill Shed. See: above you grins a full set of molars - the envy of many a toothless one. Go inside: he'll pay fifty cents a piece for sound front teeth. Don't require so much persuasion, avoid bashfulness; suffer yourself to be "drawn out," my dear Miss - !

By the way, speaking of the opera, we must not pass unnoticed such an important personage in our midst as a veritable type of Sims Reeves[177] - Alas, I knew him well." Yes, we all know this one, especially the lady patrons of Russell & Anderson's store. He comes from the old country, you know, and asserts (*upon his honor as a gentleman*) that with his highly cultivated, powerful and pleasing (?) voice he fairly enraptures the most fashionable audiences at classic concerts and small tea-parties, but more frequently a *mixed crowd* at Anderson's Hotel; they have no piano at our house, you know, besides Hiram draws a fair "sized" glass of beer for this country.

If this limb of the opera is not a sprig from Sims Reeves himself, then Spriggins[178] must have sprung from some still greater artist.

He does not like this blawsted country, and repeats this more often in one day than he does his prayers in a whole year, - of course the great trouble is the weather again, "up to your - eyes in snow, &c., &c.

Mr. S. prefers London - not that miserable village in Canada, but old London where the weather is simply delightful, between the rain, smoke and dense fog. Why, hang it all, I tell you a man can go out doors armed with a cheese-knife and carve such weather to suit himself.

We might add, for the information of Mr. S. and others of his ha! ha! stamp, that the fare across the Atlantic is now fixed at the small sum of £5 10s., and it would be a difficult matter for them to find friends enough to join the parting chorus of "Come back, Jack."

Over the way - we must not altogether ignore our neighbors over the way - scowls down upon you Mr. Macgregor's monster boot, as if it would crunch all creation beneath its heel. Ha! ha! typical of some despotic little men, but no great ones. Is it a cribbed trophy of Jack the Giant-killer's, hung up there in evidence of the truth of the nursery tale, as the friars in continental churches show you the real toe-nails of a saint in confirmation of certain miraculous cures wrought by their

---

[176] A local dentist.

[177] John Sims Reeves (1821-1900) was the foremost English operatic, oratorio and ballad tenor vocalist of the mid-Victorian era.

[178] The identity and career of this English opera singer, Mr. Spriggins, at Guelph in the 1870's, remains for future research.

patron? Is it Goliath's worn-out shoe-leather, left to undergo repair, pawned for expense of keep, and finally stuck here as a warning to forgetful customers? Can't say: it is amongst the unfathomable mysteries of things, *"Est modus in rebus,"*[179] but this rebus defies our humble intellect.

And this is Day's bookstore. Have no fear to enter; it is a favorite place of resort for all who are out at elbows.[180] Wrapped in the depths of the mighty minds long dead - pardon the lapsus,[181]

> "Die menschen-Seele stirbt doch nie,
> Sie wachst, zwar immer mehr zum licht"[182] -

you will forget all your cares, besides, it costs nothing and is respectable. Soft draperies o'erhead keep out too much of the peering light; musical boxes discourse harmony by your side, and such visions of female grace as come tripping in at the door might tempt a saint to linger.

> "But the good St. Anthony kept his eyes firmly fixed upon his book,[183]
> Shouts nor laughter, yells nor cries, could ever win away his look."

Good, good! clap that! Be amongst the saintly ones, my friend. Ah, but we hear further how the saint had been tempted with -

> "Devils with tails and devils without, devils great and devils small,[184]
> But the lovely woman with two black eyes was the greatest devil of them all."

Alack, poor humanity!

---

[179] *Est modus in rebus* (Latin) = there is a proper measure in things.

[180] "Out at elbows" meaning impoverished, tattered, shabby.

[181] Lapsus = involuntary mistake while speaking or writing; here it is quite intentional.

[182] *Die menschen...* - German: "The human soul never dies, in fact she grows ever more to the light" (translation by Nick Ford).

[183] This first line is found in the April 17, 1873 *Melbourne Punch*, page 125, referring to Anthony Trollope.

[184] This first line, in reverse order, is found in "The Old Story" in *Lectures to Working Men* by the Rev. Arthur Mursell, 1859. Page 8.

To Cynthia.[185]

Tell me, if to sin be sweet,
Can it be so bad to fall?
Better perish at thy feet,
Than, loving not, live scarce at all!

In thine eyes, if devils live,
There's a fiercer at my heart;
Half my life I'd freely give
To be blest, the other part!

Tho' perish inch by inch,
Till my heart be lost to me,
It is the stake - I will not flinch,
Yet, may I find my all in thee!

*Vamos*[186] from these hospitable portals! Have we any lawyers in Guelph? Lots, my friend. They are omnipresent, and, if not omniscient, it isn't their fault, poor creatures! They are here, there and everywhere, wherever they are wanted, and in many places where they are not. Their dens are all over the town. When not doing worse they are to be found sitting upon heaps of skulls and moth-eaten title-deeds of once broad acres, singing "fee, fi, fo, fum," only they always stop at - "fee."

What else have we of notice in the town? You are in a hurry to be off, eh? Why lots of things - lions, lions, all of 'em. The foundations of the Catholic church, for instance - a grand idea, if only it had been carried out. How few of us but have such, only they can't be dragged out with anything short of a logging chain. But no bishop, however heated with religious fervor, would ever sit perched in a puddle upon twelve feet of stone wall to preach, and no congregation would climb a board fence to attend service, and that ends the matter. There's our new school building[187], that looks so majestic from afar, and might mislead a stranger into over-estimating the intellectual calibre of our townsmen. Would you credit it - there's not a foot of play-ground! Ah, that was a miserable subterfuge of feudal times, got

---

[185] Possibly a reference to "The Ocean's Love to Cynthia," or, "The Ocean, to Cynthia," a long elegy written by Sir Walter Raleigh (1554-1618) to celebrate Queen Elizabeth I as 'Cynthia'. Or, a reference to *Cynthia: with the Unfortunate Loves of Almerin and Desdemona* (1687).

[186] Spanish for "we go."

[187] The Central School, of which only the steps up the steep incline at the end of Commercial Street survive.

up by a bloated and selfish *cela*[188]. The mind of the people shall be unshackled - the mind of the people shall soar eagle-free - the minds and bodies of the children of the people shall be enlarged, Christianized and released from the depressing thraldom of centuries by a discipline of slack-rope walking. We will put up a cable for the rising youth from the apex of Mr. Torrance's church to Mr. Wardrope's steeple! "Pshaw! I've see'd a rope afore," says one. Ah, yes, but that must have been the tight-rope. Now, don't be angry - keep your temper, my good man; you forced me to do it: you shouldn't sulk so.

The glories of Guelph are by no means exhausted. Yet, in order to heighten the effect, a few more artistic touches should be given in rapid succession. Then the full contour of the beauteous image will be apparent.

We boast a Royal Hotel, whose winged *reptilia* and ten-cent cigars testify to the justice of its claims to blue-blooded patronage. Two mammoth ledgers used to occupy the counter. We understand the present manager is one Book-less[189]. We have a chair, in common with all towns of high scholastic attainments, and it hangs up above Hazelton's store. Here the talented principal of the High School sits on Saturday mornings to expound the Platonic philosophy to his followers of the peripatetic school: - 11 A.M. sharp; bucolics invited to attend. The chair was offered to Hon. A. Crooks, as professor of Gnostics and Oriental Prestidigitomancy[190], but was declined. It is now kept for the use of such members as may have the misfortune to be unseated in the *fracas* of the coming election. It was painted green, for moral purposes, viz., that envious candidates for the "See" might see themselves literally in the color in which others see them.[191] We have a jail, as becomes a polished people. We are all polished, and as for the inmates of the jail some seem fairly greased, they are so slippery. O'Donnell was one. He slipped over the wall, stopped to black his boots, then, "folding his tent, like the Arab, he silently stole away." Still, there are many inside who have the best right there, but far from all.

We have an Agricultural Farm, outside the peaceful purlieus of our town. We are strong upon Rhubarb. The farm belongs to Government, and the soil is good, although it was once all Stone's[192].

Then comes the Temperance Hall, whose motto might be "*Semper Eadem*,"[193] referring not so much to the unreasoning arrogance of the supporters of the

---

[188] Latin for cell (prison).

[189] A play on the surname of the manager, Mr. Bookless.

[190] Prestidigitation: magic tricks performed as entertainment.

[191] i.e. inexperienced

[192] Frederick Stone

[193] *Semper Eadem*: Latin for "Ever the Same."

movement generally as to the stability of the foundation walls which, the reverse of Hannibal's soldiers, never advanced. How should they, being built upon a rotten foundation of dirty water, instead of the glorious element with which Dr. Dunlop and Mr. Galt helped to cement the original foundations of our then infant town? We have a Macdonnell street, which is no street at all, but a Rosemond's bower[194] kind of labyrinth planked with drays and offal, where the ghastly gums of moribund caninity lie turned back to give defiance at the moon! We have a Post Office, where we receive our letters, and whose boxes are ever under examination by the letters for cheques that have all mysteriously gone astray through the Post Office. Now and again the Post authorities let us have a letter; usually they let us cool our heels outside longer than Dante was kept at the gates of the Inferno, and then let us go minus. The verb "To let" is, in fact, used in a Shakspearian sense throughout. We have an English church, built conveniently upon the river's brink, with a herd of lean swine kept ready for emergencies in an adjoining meadow. We have, also, a new Canon, armed with hyper Pontifical authority, to whom the exorcism of unclean spirits is a bagatelle; the healing of a leg or the blacking of an eye, a snap of the fingers. We have an Imperial Roman Consul, next door to a pork-butcher's, who sits with his toga tucked between his knees, like Crassus of old, smoking a never-ending cutty-pipe. He hopes, by judicious fumigation, to scare away the mosquitoes, the ladies, and other dangerous creatures, which should not trench upon the dignity of the Roman empire, or aspire to sting the core of an Imperial Roman Consul's heart, or the tip of an Imperial Roman Consul's nose. We have Raymond's hurdy-gurdy factory, that was burned down some months ago. During the conflagration, the proprietor, hearing that some score of his employees were roasting in the building, ordered 500 hurdy-gurdies, placed higgle-piggledy amongst the salvage, to be arranged in rows upon the sidewalk, then, like Nero with his Christian martyrs, ordered Vale's cornet band engaged for the purpose, to grind away, until the shrieks of the victims were drowned in unhallowed revel!! This, ratepayers, is he whom you have elevated to the lofty height of School Trustee! this he who will, be Mayor of the town, and "monarch" of this peaceful community! We have the Osborn hair-pin factory, founded upon wind, maintained upon water and driven by steam. They have taken so many prizes, that no wonder proprietors and employees wear a uniformly surprised look. Perhaps the meagre abstinence diet has affected the intellects of these unfortunate men, which often lies entirely in the stomach. We have a Crowe, who occasionally crows in Council, but his crow is worse than his bite. Where all crow their loudest, it is hard for any par-

---

[194] Rosamund Clifford (before 1150-c.1176), often called "The Fair Rosamund" or the "Rose of the World," was famed for her beauty and was mistress of King Henry II of England, famous in English folklore. One tale has Henry constructing the hunting lodge at Woodstock for her and surrounding it with a garden that was a labyrinth; "Rosamund's Bower," which was pulled down when Blenheim Palace was built nearby.

ticular bird to make himself heard. We have a big Bell, whose clang is heard all over the Province, and the notes are very melodious. He "knows the wires," he does! We have Arms' machine shop: enter. Have you seen to-day's paper? There's *a file* to hand. You are ashamed to enter because of your notorious ugliness, eh? Never mind: be you ever so plain, cross his threshold, and I will show you a planer. If you feel awkward, why here's a drilling machine, pat to the purpose. Here, human arms, urged by Arms, turn out steam arms, to arm the disarmed armories and factories of the Dominion. We have a Grammar School, where the higher classics are taught the young idea for fifteen cents a lesson; a raw turnip thrown in, at noon, to stay the youthful appetite. When the cramped little intellects of pupils and tutors make it necessary, we whistle out our tamed trains of rats, who, following directions, grasp, each, his predecessor's tail in his mouth, the Principal taking up the rear, and march round the classic Rotunda, to the lively strains of "Good-bye, John." *ad obligatum* by the scholars.

We have a resort known as 'Kate's Hole,'[195] the undeniable true entrance into Purgatory. Several Mayors and Councilmen, and a dozen School Trustees went missing, and were sought for, to no purpose, until one night, after a famous oyster supper, when a councilman dreamed a dream, revealing the whole dismal truth. The result was, a deputation, a conference, minutes passed, resolutions proposed, seconded, carried, and, after these brief preliminaries, a pilgrimage to Kate's Hole. A protracted attempt to rescue *Les Miserables* from Styx, filled the chasm with briny tears, but divil (*sic*) a one came back! There they sticks!

We have public baths, upon the ancient classic model, with draperies in front, reaching below the eyes of the bather when standing. Public, public, altogether too public. Yet, what a blessing it is, that we live in the times we do! Were it otherwise, that glorious statue of Venus Aphrodite rising from the sea, might never have been chiselled, and we should have been 'chiselled' out of a noble work of art. Had the goddess, paying a flying visit to Guelph, by the 2:30 express, conceived the laudable design of bathing in the classic Speed, her doom must have been sealed upon entering our Mansions of Natation,[196] for, taking the first 'header' a side-glance from those lovely and vigilant eyes must have comprised the iron structure (*sic*) of the Eramosa Bridge, and dozens of unholy eyeballs bulls-eyeing her neighbourhood. She would never rise.

We have a descendant of, the immortal hero of Trafalgar - a Nelson - inheriting some of his illustrious predecessor's coloring, bodily, mentally, but, let's trust, not morally. O, no; we modern, thrice distilled, methodical, select sectaries have outgrown all the lusts of the flesh, all the devils which cost man so much to con-

---

[195] The location of Kate's Hole remains a mystery.

[196] Natation: the act or skill of swimming.

quer, of old. We are ultra refined, scarce flesh and blood, not at all human. Catholicity is rubbish, Christ's Church is of the elect and those are we, the salt of the earth. If any man say the salt has, will, or can, lose its savour, let him be anathema!

But our Nelson leads no forlorn hope to "choke the deadly breach" with human bodies, nor does he guide close ranks of wooden three deckers or iron turret-ships through the stormy sweep of Biscay, or over the voluptuous swell of Egyptian waters. His is our washerman, child of Afric, and very decent man. He's the boy to turn out clean shirts. Try him! Judge of our malice, kind reader, when we advertise men gratis.[197] Thought fails, memory flags, a brief breathing space must be vouchsafed us, ere, in measured, solemn cadence, we conclude the enumeration of the glories of our beloved town.

"Next," as the barber says. Why we have the Exhibition buildings, where we show fat cattle, bull-frogs, mosquitoes, pretty ankles and other healthy products of the neighbourhood. Here we bring all the honest men we can find, and seal them up in glass cases for the admiration of a less favoured outside world. We had one and a half this year; the doctors, in consultation with the parsons, coming to the determination that the exhibition in public of two full grown perfect specimens of physical and moral manhood might precipitate the Millennium. They resorted to amputation. Then, this must not be overlooked, the river Speed, down by the Dundas Bridge[198], with its picturesque windings and warpings between hazel-clad banks, and over gleaming pebbles. - Here resort the love-sick and the life-weary, some of whom have cast themselves into the treacherous fluid embraces of the chief-syren of the waters. Others have returned with braces broken, or waterfalls dripping - as the nature of the case might determine - to live and chew the beneficial cud of sober reflection. Here the bull-frogs do congregate in the 'Spa' season, and muskrats scratch their sleek backs upon the pendant thorn. Here, along this devious, serpentine channel, the Argonauts pass, laden with many a 'Golden Fleece' - to that blest spot, ycleped[199] Paradise, whence, having disposed of lots of biscuits, cakes and soda-water, they embark for home.

Ah, lovely Speed! How often, looking down into thy glassy depths of waters, laden, as I was, with care and travail, have I felt like Prometheus bound to the rock, from which a harsh creed forbade him release. How often turned from the contemplation of my petty troubles to the solemn silence of thy lucid breast, till syren and nereid[200] grew into being before my gaze, and I muttered, with him of old -

---

[197] The author supports the freedom of all humans and asks the reader to keep this in mind when judging his "malice" towards aspects of Guelph culture.

[198] Now Gordon Street bridge.

[199] Archaic form of called or named.

[200] Nereids: sea nymphs in ancient Greek mythology.

"Ho dios aither kai tachupteroi pnoai
Potamon te pagai! &c. &c."[201]

## TO SPEDA.

Flow, River, flow;
Like the leaf o'er thy calm breast sailing
Is the soul that is wedded to trifles below
When honor and duty are hailing.
For the leaf floats along in full view of the shore
With never an effort and never a goal,
Till its fibres be torn and the combat be o'er:
God grant that so craven be never my soul!

Flow, River, flow;
Like the weed thro' thy soft vest peering
Is the soul that stands firm when the north winds blow,
Whilst storm-steeds around it are rearing, -
For the weed bows its neck just enough to the blast,
Yet suffers no power to rivet control;
Then, proud in its courage, it stoutly holds fast:
To the good, to the true, so hold, ever, my soul!"

We have a literary office, above Herod's drug store,[202] where "Looking Glasses"[203] are electrotyped, and "Horsetamers" broken in, to suit the fickle public. Mr. Megaffin,[204] proprietor, is an enterprising young man, and promises well - for the Lunatic Asylum. He lives upon blue-pills, courteously carried upstairs into the editorial sanctum of the "Family Journal," by the junior druggist below. Since the recent development of alarming symptoms, caused by the sloughing off from the editorial brain of that famous article, headed - "I'm going to be a Millionaire!"[205] chloride

---

[201] From *Prometheus Bound*, formerly thought to be by Aeschylus.

[202] Formerly at the corner of Cork and Wyndham Street, north side.

[203] Unknown publication by A. H. Megaffin. See Appendix E.

[204] *Tachyhippodamia or, The new secret of taming horses*. By Willis J. Powell and John Solomon Rarey. 1874. Megaffin, Guelph.

[205] Unidentified article.

of gold has been added to the regimen, upon the principle - *similia similibus curantur.*[206] However: his books sell, and the symptoms may abate, as the sales decrease. May he have a long illness.

And now, dear reader, by way of redeeming the character of our tete-a-tete from the charge of monotony, we interpolate the standard staidness of our text with some choice flowers of poesy.

### DAVIDSON'S FOLLY.

### A POEM, IN ENGLISH VERSE.

There's just a little bit of fun
To do with Charlie Davidson,
Who "blows his horn" - true councilman -
When decent folk are slumbering.

So came it that, on Monday last,*
Bluff Charlie wagged his tongue too fast,
Declaimed, with fire too hot to last.
The By-Law for House Numbering.

Because no Town Plan had been fyled,
This cholery councilman was "riled;"
His virtuous breast with fury biled
Against the Guelph Directory.

Quoth he - "My chums, who'd be the fool
To crouch 'neath Charlton's iron rule?
I never will be slave or tool,
Nor let that cock crow 'victory.'

"I'll have no number to my door,
I'll keep my sidewalks clean no more,
Tho' the Law's myrmidons should pour
Like locusts from Poughumpery.

---

[206] Latin: "similar things take care of similar things" or "like cures like" (Paracelsus; 16th century).

"I - I - I - gentlemen, I'm riled,
And, tho' in H--l for it I'm briled,
Yet never be my house defiled
With Charlton's licensed trumpery.

"As for the Institute Mechanic,
It is a fraud, vast and Titanic,
And asinine, if not Satanic,
As bad as this Directory.

"I move we turn it out of doors,
That none who spell shall walk these floors.
In short, we want no learned boors,
To crow at Charlton's victory!"

The last word spoke, the Council rise,
Each man with horror in his eyes,
And pity battling with surprise,
In view of such insanity.

Each awe struck member, as he rose,
Coughed thrice, spat twice, and blew his nose,
Then grandly from the Hall he goes;
So ends this dull inanity.

*See Council proceedings for Oct. 4th.

Refreshing, is it not? - Truth always is. We hope Mr. Davidson may find it so..
Guelph, Oct. 5th, 1875.                                           DI."

\*\*\*

# XX

# 𝔄. 𝔈. 𝔏. 𝔗RELEAVEN

## FLOURISHED 1877

A.E.L. Treleaven wrote the poem "Guelph's Fiftieth Anniversary" in 1877 and published it as a four page pamphlet in that year.[207] This rare pamphlet was printed at the Herald Steam Printing Establishment, Guelph.[208]

## GUELPH'S FIFTIETH ANNIVERSARY

Just fifty years ago to-day,
    Noble Galt and Dunlop stood -
With brandy flask and powder horn -
    Within a pathless wood;
An Indian cabin nestled there,
    Offering shelter from the storm:
Gladly they sought its humble shade,
    To rest each weary'd form.

Galt struck the monarch of the wilds,
    With strong manhood's earnest might;
Dunlop, Prior and the wood men fell'd
    It, on that thrice-honored night:
For good King George[209], our patron saint,
    Made it famous in his day -
When chivalry and brave knighthood
    Held firm undisputed sway.

---

[207] See Johnson 1977:342 and Wiljer 1990:64. Johnson does not mention Treleaven and ascribes the poem to "Anonymous."

[208] See Appendix C.

[209] King George IV reigned 1820-1830.

Great Shakspeare, the prince of poets,
    Entered this blooming world;
On that same day, in after years[210] -
    His life in death was furled.
Galt gave England's royal honored name
    To the then far distant town:
Never let ignoble acts or deeds
    Tarnish its bright renown.

Let us take a retrospective glance
    Over the then and now:
Then forests, Indians and wild beasts,
    Alone crown'd nature's brow;
Guelph of to-day in honor stands -
    A bright imperial gem,
Which our Queen need ne'er blush to own
    As a star in her diadem.

Her Churches, gems of modern art,
    With their lofty sparkling spires,
Leads one to hope that Christian grace,
    Noble thoughts and deeds inspires;
Her Hospitals are doing a noble work -
    Where her sick meet tender care
From the sisters and nurses - woman's hands
    Render loving duties there.

Her Schools, magnificent structures, stand
    Wherein intelligence and grace
Are cultured by an efficient band,
    Bright ornaments in any place;
Her Agricultural College, the farmer's pride -
    There their sons are wisely taught
The science of tilling dear old Earth,
    With such wealth and beauty fraught.

---

[210] William Shakespeare was baptized 26 April, 1564, and died 23 April, 1616. His actual birthdate is not know, but traditionally observed on 23 April, Saint George's Day.

A home from the aged and the maim,
    Will shortly lift its head -
An asylum for distress and pain,
    There the helpless may have bread;
Her Ministers, gentle Christian men,
    Working in their Master's name:
Striving to lift poor straying souls
    From the depths of sin and shame.

Her Doctors, men of scientific skill,
    Stand foremost in the ranks;
For this, their gentle healing art,
    We yield them warmest thanks.
Her Lawyers, men of scholastic lore,
    Winning laurels and renown:
From our Senate Halls, we hear the voice
    Of a resident of our Town.

Her Editorial staff are managed by
    Brilliant minds and willing hands,
Assisted by telegraph and steam engines,
    Bringing in news from foreign lands.
Her Courts and Councils are govern'd well,
    By men of good common sense,
Who give their influence and time,
    Her means and justice to dispense.

Her Merchants, kindly courteous men,
    Stand ready, with bows and smiles,
To lead us gently through the maze
    Of subtle fashion's changing wiles.
Her Mechanics, men of honest worth,
    A mighty bulwark stand,
With gifted minds and simple faith,
    A tower of strength in our land.

Her Farmers, sturdy sons of toil -
  To them we yield the palm
For independence and sweet peace,
  And fair primeval calm.
Her brave Volunteers - God bless them! -
  Stand ready to defend
Their homes at a moment's warning,
  And their Queen - the people's friend.

Her Daughters fill an honored place -
  Fair maidens, and blooming wives
And mothers; Heaven's blessing rest
  On their self-sacrificing lives.
Then come forth, ye aged veterans,
  Ye early settlers come:
Enjoy the peace and pleasure
  Flowing from each pleasant home.

Many friends have fallen in our midst
  This is the lot of man:
To love, to labor and to die -
  Life is such a little span.
Brave Galt, the founder of our Town.
  Now sleeps on Scotia's shore;
His kind colleagues of those days
  Are known on earth no more.

Thus our retrospect is sadly tinged
  By changes and dire decay:
Who will be here, of this vast crowd,
  To greet Guelph's Centennial day?
Fling sadness aside, let each glad heart
  Rejoice in laughter and song;
Let kind good will and merry cheer -
  The joyous hours prolong.

Three cheers for our beloved Queen!
　　Three cheers for our patron saint!
And three times three for dear old Guelph,
　　May her brave hearts never faint!
To God let each glad homage bring
　　On this bright auspicious day;
Long may it in our memories ring,
　　Fragrant as the breath of May.

\* \* \*

# XXI

## Charles C. Foster

### Flourished 1879

Little more of Charles C. Foster (born c.1809) is known other than his poem "The City of Guelph," which was composed in 1879, on the 52nd anniversary of the city's foundation.

### THE CITY OF GUELPH
("Writen (*sic*) for the Guelph Mercury, on the 23rd of April, 1879")

I was but a youth when first I left
My quiet village home,
In search of rest and solitude
Through pathless woods to roam.
'Twas a lovely day in Autumn
Just at the hour of eventide,
That I pitched my tiny tent
By the river's wooded side.
The vast unbroken forest
Stood thick on hill and dale,
No pathway through its shadows
Save perchance an Indian trail.
The grand old trees of Wellington,
Stood in all their native grace,
While no sounds save those of nature
Broke the silence of the place.
The river flowing southward
The wooded hills between,
And anon an Indian's birch canoe
Came softly down the stream.
I gazed from yonder hillside
As long as I could see,
And then knelt down and cut my name

In the bark of a maple tree.
Some days I lingered near the spot
    Or, in hunting, roved about,
And tried my luck in a neighbouring stream
    For the famous speckled trout.
But the chilling winds of Autumn
    Spoke of winter coming then,
So I left this sylvan solitude
    And sought the haunts of men.

As time rolled on a summer came
    When I had time to spare,
So to my well-known woodland haunts
    I quickly did repair.
I stood once more upon the hill
    Where I so oft before had been,
And as I gazed around me thought
    How changed is all the scene.
A rustic bridge now spans the stream
    By which I loved to roam,
And o'er the hills around me
    Stands many a woodland home.
The grand old trees of Wellington
    Lie felled upon the ground,
While many a woodman's axe awakes
    The sleeping echoes round.
A log built hamlet nestling
    Close by the river's side,
While signs of habitation
    Lie round me far and wide.
But the place has lost its charm for me
    I'll stay no longer here,
For the lovely woodland spot has made
    A home for the pioneer.

Long years have rolled away since then,
    But I once more climb the hill,
And as I gaze about me see
    A change far greater still.
The little log built village
    Has long since passed away,
And on its site so proud and grand
    A city stands to-day.
The spires of noble churches
    Point upwards to the sky,
While from many a stately building
    The flags and streamers fly.
I hear the boom of cannon
    And the strains of many a band,
While signs of mirth and pleasure
    Are round on every hand.
The mingled sound of voices
    With the tread of countless feet,
Of the throngs of pleasure seekers
    Who crowd through each handsome street.
And sounds of soft sweet melody
    With the clash of many bells,
Wafted on the soft spring air
    Of mirth and music tells.
I hear the shriek of engines
    The horse of modern time,
While electric wires flash forth the news
    From many a distant clime.
So time has wrought its changes
    As the years have rolled away,
I note it all so plainly
    While I view the scene to-day.
And time has worked a change with me
    'Twixt the present time and then,
For now the youth in years has seen
    A good three score and ten.[211]
And time will still work changes

---

[211] A score is 20, therefore "three score and ten" is 70. Foster seems to be referring to his age as of writing this poem - born c.1809.

Alas! and perhaps too soon,
When we who have watched its progress
Lie silent in the tomb.

\* \* \*

# XXII

## "Madge"

**FLOURISHED 1879**

The identity and career of "Madge" remains unknown. Whether the pseudonym "Madge" stands for Margaret also remains unclear. The sole poem to survive from this versifier is the fragment below, written at Guelph on 23 May, 1879.

### [FRAGMENT: TITLE UNKNOWN]
("Guelph, May 23, 1879" Printed in the *Mercury* 14 June, 1879)

> ...learned,
> And sun and stars for evermore have set,
> The things which our weak judgements here have
> spurned,
> The things o'er which we grieved with lashes wet,
> Will flash before us, out of life's dark night:
> As stars shine most in deeper tints of blue,
> And we shall see how all God's plans were right,
> And how what seemed reproof was love most true.
>
> And we shall see how, while we frown and sigh,
> God's plans go on as best for you and me;
> How, when we called, He heeded not our cry,
> Because His wisdom to the end could see.
> And e'en as prudent parents dissallow
> Too much of sweet to craving babyhood,
> So God, perhaps, is keeping from us now
> Life's sweetest things because it seemeth good.

And if sometimes commingled with life's wine,
　　We find the wormwood and rebel and shrink,
Be sure a wiser hand than yours or mine
　　Pours out this potion for our lips to drink.
And if some friend we love is lying low,
　　Where human kisses cannot reach his face,
Oh, do not blame the loving Father so,
　　But wear your sorrow with obedient grace.

And you shall shortly know that lengthened breath
　　Is not the sweetest gift God sends His friend,
And that sometimes the sable pall of death
　　Conceals the fairest boon His love can send.
If we could push ajar the gates of life,
　　And stand within and all God's workings see,
We could interpret all this doubt and strife,
　　And for each mystery find a fitting key.

But not to-day. Then be content, poor heart,
　　God's plans, like lillies pure and white, unfold;
We must not tear the close-shut leaves apart;
　　Time will reveal the calyxes of gold.
And if thro' patient toil we reach the land
　　Where tired feet with sandals loose may rest,
Then we shall clearly know and understand,
　　I think that we will say, "God knew the best.'

　　"And there shall be no more death; neither
sorrow, nor crying: neither shall there be any
more pain; for the former things are passed
away."

*　*　*

# XXIII

## 𝔍.𝔍.𝔐.

**FLOURISHED 1881**

The identity of J.F.M. remains unknown. This versifier's poem "The Strange Wish" was written in 1881 for the Guelph *Herald*. A relative may be the unknown "Cammy" (i.e., Camelia) referred to.

### THE STRANGE WISH
("Written for the Herald" Printed 6 October, 1881)

Oh would that once again were here,
    With all its weight of sorrow fraught,
The day when o'er "Our Cammy's" bier,
    We wept as one in heart and thought.

Firm clasping each the other's hand,
    Each wishing but the other's good,
A weeping, love-united band,
    Beside that coffined form we stood.

Our hearts must break, we simply said,
    Ah! little did we children think -
That time would heal, and mem'ry fade,
    And snap our love chain link from link.

That hearts which then o'erflowed with love,
    Could e'er become estranged and dead,
Too hard to break - too cold to move -
    The tenderness of yore all fled.

The paths diverge - our wish is vain,
        For now we know that never more,
As one in heart and thought again,
        We'll stand upon this earthly shore.

\*\*\*

# XXIV

## 𝕸ARGARET 𝕭EATRICE 𝕭URROWS
## (NÉE 𝕬NDERSON)

### 20 AUGUST, 1841, PORTSOY, BANFFSHIRE, SCOTLAND - AFTER 1900, OTTAWA, CANADA

Margaret Beatrice Burrows was the daughter of Thomas Anderson. Her brother, Thomas Anderson, was a journalist with the Guelph *Mercury*, and he died here in 1866.[212] At some point before 1884 she lived in Ottawa and came to stay in Guelph for the summer season of that year, probably residing with friends James Innes and his wife Helen. Her poem "Memories of Guelph" was written for Helen Innes, and James, the proprietor of the *Mercury* at this date, printed it in the paper on September 20, 1884. Our knowledge of this versifier rests upon a now rare 1900 publication, *Selections from Scottish Canadian Poets*.[213]

## MEMORIES OF GUELPH
("Inscribed to Mrs James Innes"[214])

Low in the west the great day orb descends,
While I, with eyes enraptured, gaze upon
A scene of passing beauty, sky and cloud
Lit with a thousand parting rays that flash
And quiver in the evening atmosphere.
Well worthy of the royal name it bears,
The city lies before me, stretching out

---

[212] Clark 1900:268. See Further Reading: Clark 1900.

[213] Guelph Historical Society Publications: Volume IV, Number 12, 1964 [unnamed compiler] claims that *Selections from Scottish Canadian Poets* (1900) states: "this poem was printed in *The Guelph Mercury*, September 25, 1884" and cites this as though it comes from page 268 of the 1900 publication. *Selections* (Pp. 268-277) makes no such claim. In addition, the unnamed compiler of the 1964 Guelph Historical Society publication has the incorrect date for when the poem appeared in the *Mercury*. The poem was in fact printed in the *Mercury* on 20 September, 1884 (verified by checking the *Mercury* microfilm archives at the Guelph Public Library). Later, the mistake was unfortunately transmitted into the article by Wiljer (1990:64).

[214] Helen Innes. This poem appears in *Selections from Scottish Canadian Poets* (1900) on page 276-277.

To east and west its lusty, youthful arms;
Like ancient Athens, resting on the hills,
On every side its schools of learning stand;
The spires of many churches pierce the sky;
Fair villas nestle in the leafy shade
Of feathery elm and stately, sheltering oak,
Of straight-limbed poplar and the maple grand,
Which sways alike elastic through the storm,
Or glows with beauty in the autumn moon -
Its leaves blend, emblematic, with the rose
Of England fair, the *fleur de lis* of France,
The bearded thistle from stern Scotland's shores
And shamrock green, to fitly represent
A diverse people, yet united - one
In courage, wealth and strength - destined to be
A solid, vigorous nation in themselves.
Like vein of steadfast friendship, through the vale
The quiet Speed meanders on its way,
Serene and peaceful, like the honest lives
Of those who find their homes upon its banks.
Fair Guelph, fair scene, reflected through the years
By memory's magic mirror to my view,
Thy beauty back shall come to feast my soul
My pulses stir with gratitude to those
Dear friends and kind who made my summer stay
Within thy borders more than pleasure rare -
A picture that shall fade not with the flowers
Of seasons yet to come.

Ottawa, 8th July, 1884                    M.B.B.

\*\*\*

# XXV

## Anonymous Guelph Tourists

**1884**

The poem "Elora" appeared in the *Guelph Daily Mercury* on 6 September, 1884, with the explanation "Joint Production of Tourists on Their Way Home. Guelph, Sept. 4, 1884." September 4th of 1884 was a Thursday.

### Elora

To see Elora's far-famed den,
    From Guelph our party went one day,
Our purpose to explore the glen,
    Each darksome cave and stony way.

The rocks in rugged grandeur rose,
    Where Irvine's foaming waters rolled,
We saw great trees their branches close,
    O'er cliffs where eagles built of old.

We drank the waters of the spring,
    Soft welling from the mountain block,
We heard the merry school boy sing,
    While scaling high the copse clad rock.

We climbed the steep and rugged stair,
    Hearing below the waters dash,
And from the bridge in sunny air,
    We saw the wild bird's pinions flash.

We followed wild and devious ways,
  Plucking the wild flower and the fern,
'Mid pines through which in other days,
  Brushed the red Indian, plumed and stern.

From mossy trunk at mouth of cave
  Wes saw itself the green toad fling,
While up the rock like stormer brave,
  We saw Virginia's creeper spring.

We sat beneath the shady trees,
  The broken waters babbling by,
And ate our biscuit with our cheese,
  Wishing the cooling fountain nigh.

As home we went, when all was o'er,
  The carriage wheeling on the way,
The moon the landscape silvered o'er,
  And Jehu did all skill display.

And visions fair of cups and tea,
  Floated before or[215] weary eyes,
And Auntie dear, we plainly see,
  Preparing sumptuous supplies.

       \* \* \*

---

[215] 1884 printing error for "our".

# XXVI

## 𝕿HOMAS 𝕷AIDLAW

### 1825, ROXBURGHSHIRE, SCOTLAND -
### 1902, GUELPH, ONTARIO, CANADA.
### RESIDED IN GUELPH 1831-1902

Thomas Laidlaw was born in Roxburghshire, Scotland, 1825, and died in Guelph City in 1902, age 77 years. He married Janet Martin, who died in 1892, aged 69 years. Originally, Thomas Laidlaw came to Canada with his parents in 1831. He purchased, and settled on his "Paisley Block" farm of 150 acres, and lived there until retiring to Guelph City in 1885. Aside from attending the Cowan School, he was a self-educated man, and became a writer of some note. Besides contributing extensively to the press, he wrote and published: "Old Concession Road," "Sprigs of Heather," and "The Old Cattle Bell, or Days of Long Ago." He was an Elder in the Presbyterian church, a Liberal in politics, and of a clever, interesting personality. He was Bard of the Guelph St. Andrew's Society, and at their annual meeting, always contributed a poem on "Old Scotia" or "Scotch Life," with which he was familiar.[216]

The Frontispiece to the 1899 edition of Laidlaw's *The Old Concession Road*, and the verse at the beginning of the chapter "Trout Fishing"[217]:

> The speckled trout, when we were boys,
> That finned the shady streams,
> And glanced above the sandy bars,
> Are flashing through our dreams.

---

[216] *Historical Atlas of the County of Wellington, Ontario*. Toronto: Historical Atlas Publishing Co., 1906.

[217] Laidlaw 1899:29

Verse at the beginning of the chapter "The Sugar Camp"[218]:

> Stars twinkle from a summer sky,
> And through the pale moonlight,
> The sweet clear notes of whippoorwill
> Enrich the silent night.
> But list! the far resounding horn
> Is doubling through the woods;
> Some hapless one has lost his way
> In pathless solitudes.

Verse at the beginning of the chapter "A Sabbath in the Early Days"[219]:

> A day of rest, no grating note
>     Disturbs this brooding spell,
> No, voice save nature's blending with
>     The tinkling cattle-bell;
> The weary prize this precious gift -
>     A holy Sabbath calm,
> The reverend woods their voices lift
>     And sing their hymn and psalm.

Verse at the beginning of the chapter "A Raising 'Bee'"[220]:

> In groupings where the "grog-boss" sat,
>     What zestful tales were told,
> What news discussed of other lands,
>     Albeit rather old.

---

[218] Laidlaw 1899:10

[219] Laidlaw 1899:15

[220] Laidlaw 1899:19

Verse at the beginning of the chapter "The Ox"[221]:

> Sagacious ox, mute honest beast,
>> We long together wrought;
> How wise thou wert! yet thou hast left
>> With all you ever thought.

Verse at the beginning of the chapter "The Old By-Roads"[222]:

> The old by-tracks, we knew them well,
>> They served a day of need.
> Where did they lead to; who could tell
>> To where they did not lead?

Verse at the beginning of the chapter "The New Year"[223]:

> In viewless dress, through forest deep
> The old year glides away,
> We greet the new with brimming cup,
> Our spirits fresh and gay;
> We lead across the plain rough floor
> In light subduing dusk,
> The heart beats time to love and joy,
> The feet to "Money Musk".[224]

---

[221] Laidlaw 1899:22

[222] Laidlaw 1899:25

[223] Laidlaw 1899:32

[224] The reel "Money Musk," Op.815 is by Charles Grobe (c.1817-1879). First published in 1857 by Oliver Ditson & Co.

Verse at the beginning of the chapter "The Old Log School House"[225]:

> Away far off through greying mists
>     Of years that intervene,
> The old log school house still exists
>     With us a living scene;
> And still to us the native woods
>     Do fling their shadows grey
> Across its low, flat roof and still
>     We hear their organs play.

Verse at the beginning of the chapter "A Communion Season"[226]:

> Concessioners in simple form,
>     Within that little room,
> Commemorate the death which paid
>     Their penalty of doom;
> And tender thoughts fit to the time
>     When on yon Sabbath day
> They drank of the communion cup
>     With dear ones far away.

Verse at the beginning of the chapter "A Family Gathering"[227]:

> See, some on foot come in the lane,
>     And now we see a sleigh,
> The dear old homestead greets them with
>     A happy New Years Day -
> The great red glowing back-log burns
>     As in the days of old,
> And we, in circle round the hearth
>     A grand re-union hold.

---

[225] Laidlaw 1899:35

[226] Laidlaw 1899:38

[227] Laidlaw 1899:42

Verse at the beginning of the chapter "Our Fathers, Where Are They?"[228]:

> Our pioneers, who in the woods
>> The little shanty reared,
> Our widowed hearts will nevermore
>> Be with their presence cheered,
> No, nevermore their voices hear
>> In sadness or in glee,
> All still in death, and only now
>> A fading memory.

## THE CUTTING OF THE FIRST TREE IN GUELPH

(From Laidlaw's *The Old Concession Road*)

> The sun had set - an April day,
> Was blending with an evening gray,
> That softly through the forest crept;
> The stillness of the centuries slept
> In wild retreats, and undisturbed
> The native haunts of beast and bird.
> A lifted axe! an era's doom,
> Is knelling through the forest gloom,
> And when at length, with crash and swell,
> The old historic maple fell,
>> With echoes wide renewed,
> All to the scene reflection gave,
> As men beside an open grave
>> Do feel in soul subdued.
>
> Then by the fallen Titan's side,
> That erst had towered in forest pride,
>> They drank in happy mood,
> Success to Guelph in *usquebac*[229],
> Success on that her natal day,
>> Amid the native wood.

---

[228] Laidlaw 1899:48

[229] Usquaebach was derived from the ancient Gaelic phrase, "uisge beatha" meaning water of life, from which the word "whisky" is derived. Robert Burns immortalized it in his poem *Tam O'Shanter*, with the line "Wi Usquaebae, we'll face the de'il (devil)". From 1768 to 1842 it was a single malt whisky.

In vestal light the forest threw,
Its branches to a stainless blue,
As wearily in from other lands,
The fathers came like pilgrim bands,
From travel soiled; and fain were they
At length their flagging steps to stay.

A change is seen, as witnesses where
The hammer shakes the burdened air,
In alters[230] to the Triune raised,
As seemeth best where God is praised;
In streets that in perspective fade,
Where erst would fall the forest shade;
In living men, who recognize
The social link, the kindred ties
That make us one; in law whose reign
The arm of justice doth sustain.

'Tis well! yet, lured by fancy's ray
To native scenes, in thought we stray
And picture heights, now city crowned,
Superbly girt with forest round
That drowsily in the valleys stood;
While winding through the silent wood,
The nameless river rippling swept
Its rocky bed, where cedars crept
Close to its edge and heard the wash
Of waters through the silence lash.

In deep recesses, still and coy,
The leafy summer lurked in joy,
And breathed in zephyrs through the vast
Umbrageous wood that softly cast
Subduing shade, a stillness lay
In keeping with the chast'ned day -
A brooding calm that drowsily weighed
And hung o'er all; deer meekly strayed

---

[230] altars

And herbage cropped at ease, and graced
With antler crest their native waste.

And flushing sunsets bathed the woods
And sank in distant solitudes,
As west'ring up the valleys crept
The dusky night, that dark'ning kept,
Till fancy to the ear would bring
The beatings of her murky wing,
While through the gloom, the silent stars
Looked calmly twixt the rifted bars
Of ebon cloud; and up the height
The owl shot through the silent night -
Her weird too-whoo, that dying fell
On silence in the lonely dell,
And strewing winds with sullen moan,
Wailed through the forest vast and lone
As summer fled; on forests bare
Snow fluttered through the thin cold air,
While seasons rolled - yea, centuries swept
Unheeded past, no record kept
Except in rings concentric, grained
On aged trunks, that long had strained
And wrestled with the storm that lashed
Their twisted boughs, and thus were dashed,
     Till on the silence fell
The stalwart maple to its doom,
That surged in echoes through the gloom,
     An era's passing knell;
Adown the intervening years,
Our quick'ned fancy ever hears,
     A muffled crash and swell.

## TO THE RIVER SPEED

(From Laidlaw's *The Old Concession Road*)

Pellucid Speed, the years are few
Since on your banks the forest threw
Unbroken shade, and wild flowers grew,
And clamb'ring creepers swung;
The spell of ages round them lay
Unbroken, as you rolled away
      All silent and unsung.
Fain would we trace each misty scene,
With all the changes that have been
Since first the foot of white man prest
Your wooded slopes, by nature dress'd;
To twilight ages, dim and pale,
When starting down the silent vale
      Your onward course began;
Here through a swampy level led,
There rippling down a stony bed,
      And murmuring as you ran.

Enshrouded all! no annals tell
How forests rose and forests fell,
And were renewed; then in decay
Again, like others, passed away.
Yet in those silent years remote,
What dim romantic visions float;
The Indian, then in haughty pride,
Would roam in freedom by your side,
Then by the plashy[231] brink with care
He set the crafty trap and snare,
Or through the slumb'ring forest sped
With eagle-eye and stealthy tread,
In keen pursuit to track the game
That fell before his practised aim;
And when the dusky shades of night
Stole through the woods and dimm'd his sight,

---

[231] watery

He with unerring foot retraced
The trackless way - the leafy waste -
To where his lonely wigwam stood,
Its curling smoke seen through the wood.
His wants appeased, with hungry zest
He wearily laid him down to rest,
    While all around was still.
No sound fell on his slumb'ring ear,
Except your waters rippling near,
The hoot of owl, or quick and clear
    The notes of whipporwill.

Those scenes are past, and scenes to-day,
Like former scenes, shall pass away,
And in the ever deep'ning shade
Of years to dim remembrance fade;
Still youth shall in your shallows lave,
And herds shall drink your limpid wave,
And moonbeams on your waters play
That then, as now, shall break away
    Adown the pleasant vale.
On, ever on, your current tends,
Until your happy murmur blends
    With nature's dying wail.

## ON SEEING AN INDIAN MOTHER CONVEYING A CHILD'S COFFIN DOWN THE STREETS OF GUELPH

(From Laidlaw's *The Old Concession Road*)[232]

Bleak clouds floated over the sky, dark arraying,
    Snow covered the street and the landscape away,
As a poor Indian mother was lonely conveying
    A coffin she drew on a rude-fashioned sleigh;
For death in the wigwam had turned it to sighing,
Papoose's pale dust in its rude shroud was lying,
The spirit beyond where yon dark clouds are flying,
    In realms where the red man shall wander for aye.

---

[232] Hugh Douglass (c.1963) notes that this poem is by "T.S. - T.J. Starret, Garafraxa," in 1876, but that it also appears as Laidlaw's in that writer's *The Old Concession Road*.

Cold looks were cast on the dark, swarthy mother[233],
    Few knew her state, nor were mindful to know;
None turned aside, with the heart of a brother,
    In this, her bereavement, their pity to show.
To a valley she went, where a streamlet was wending,
Where the smoke of the wigwam rose upward, ascending
Through the tall forest trees, that around it were bending,
    And sighing a dirge o'er the ashes below.

Away from the wigwam, papoosie conveying,
    They scooped out a grave from the snow-covered ground;
Then ere departing, their last tribute paying,
    They chanted the death song in weird strains around,
Alone in the forest papoosie lies sleeping,
Where the night-hawk and owl lonely vigil are keeping,
With the wild wintry wind through the tall branches sweeping,
    Far from the place where the tribesmen are found.

Yet, may that mother, in her heart-felt emotion,
    As she thinks of her babe, drop the sad silent tear
Shade of a race, that from ocean to ocean,
    Must vanish till nought of a remnant appear
Once majestic to roam through their dark forests waving
The storm and the tempest alike proudly braving,
From the hand of the pale-face no boon humbly craving -
    Disdaining to plead, and a stranger to fear.

## WORKS:

Thomas Laidlaw 1879. *The Old Concession Road*. Guelph: O. E. Turnbull, Printer and Binder. Reprinted in 1899.

Thomas Laidlaw 1895. *Sprigs O' Heather for Scottish Gatherings*. Guelph: Mercury Electric Press

Thomas Laidlaw 1899. *In the Long Ago or The Days of the Cattle Bell*. Guelph: The Mercury Electric Press

---

[233] Hinds (1967) thought there may have been a connection between this Laidlaw poem and a local legend regarding an Indian mother, her child, and her husband Isaac Sky. When Sky 'went on hunting trips she stayed in a camp near the Speed River.' See Further Reading.

Thomas Laidlaw's notebook of poems dating to c.1871 is held in the Wellington County Museum archives: Accession Number A1995.62. The poems include:

"The Conquest of Canada Shansoa;" "Komoka;" "An Indian Legend;" "The Braves of the Pen;" "The Wail of the Indian Chief;" "Confederation Canada;" "The Havana Cigar;" "Samuel and Saul;" "Israel at the Red Sea;" "Morning Prayer;" "A Glimpse of Man;" "A Scene on the Mississippi;" "Verses to the Little Boy Who Had Received the Name of the Author;" "My Lizzie;" "The Isthmus of Time;" "The Life Boat;" "Interception."

\*\*\*

# XXVII

## 𝕵ames 𝕲ay

24 March, 1810, Brattan Clovelly, Devonshire, England -
1891, Guelph
Self-Proclaimed Poet Laureate of Canada

James Gay audaciously proclaimed himself to be the Poet Laureate of Canada. Be that as it may, he holds a special place in the history of Guelph versifiers. It is generally acknowledged that the quality of his verse is "good bad,"[234] but that his work "deserves to be taken seriously."[235] With the advantage of hindsight, it is now possible to consider Gay as suffering from a mental health condition known as Obsessive Compulsive Rhyming Disorder, where the symptoms manifest as repetitive rhymes spoken to relieve anxiety. In a letter from Charles Canniff James to Lawrence J. Burpee, the latter described Gay as always speaking in rhyme.[236] Gay's bold self-proclamation as a poet on a par with Lord Alfred Tennyson, and touting himself as Canada's Poet Laureate, further reveal qualities akin to delusions of grandeur. Therefore, if we view Gay's verses as the products of these conditions, it is not altogether fair to label his poetry as doggerel. There may be similarities between Gay's poetaster efforts and those of William Topaz McGonagall (1825-1902)[237] - a Scottish doggerel poet, best known for his 1880 poem "The Tay Bridge Disaster," and likely on the "autism-Asperger's spectrum."[238] Nonetheless, Gay's own output may perhaps instead be reassessed as relating to early Modernist and Absurdist poetry, but this is left for future literary scholarship. Certainly, his verses are unique.

James Gay stated that he began writing poetry "more or less" since he was 61 years old, i.e. 1871. He identifies his association with "my Brother John Gay A Devonshire Poet," after including among his other "brothers" the major Scottish and English poets (Robbie Burns, Lord Byron, William Cooper, Shakespeare, Thomas Moore and Milton). John Gay was the English poet and dramatist born 30 June, 1685 at Barnstaple in Devon - died December 4, 1732 in London, and best remembered as the author of *The Beggar's*

---

[234] Colombo and Singer 1996:Preface.

[235] *Ibid.*

[236] Deacon 1927:19; Wiljer 1990:59.

[237] Thank you to Ed Butts for drawing my attention to this.

[238] Norman Watson and Christopher Hart agreeing with Norman Watson in the *Sunday Times*, 7 November 2010.

*Opera* (1728). A genealogical connection is not yet known that satisfactorily connects James to John Gay.

James Gay stated: "I am From the Parish of Brattan Clovelly Devonshire." Bratton Clovelly is a village in Lifton Hundred, eight miles west-northwest of Okehampton, in west Devon, England. This is not the more famous Devonshire coastal village of Clovelly. The Bratton Clovelly Protestation Return of 1641/42 includes a John Gaye.[239] Further, the following Gays are listed in the Bratton Clovelly Parish Register, for burials between 1837 and 1907:

John Gay, 76 years old [born ~1763], buried 12 April, 1839
Robert Strong Gay, 3 years old [born ~1848], buried 7 June, 1851

Bill Moore[240] included Gay in his *Words That Taste Good* (1987): "One of those lesser poets, James Gay. He lived in Guelph, and was determinedly loyal and royal...He wrote to the great Tennyson, in 1882, at the height of that worthy's fame, in this way:

A poet's mind is clear and bright, No room for hatred, malice or spite.

And further suggested that the two of them were pretty well on a par:

I do not know whether a baron or a poet laureate gets any wages in England. In Canada there is no pay.

He went on with:

It is a solemn thing to reflect that I am the link connecting our great countries. I hope when I am gone another may raise up... ."[241]

The eccentricities of Gay were noted in the following item from the Guelph *Mercury & Advertiser* (quoting the Hamilton *Spectator*), on 23 June, 1884:

The Poet Gay of Guelph was in the city on Friday, and favored the *Spectator* with a card. The old gentleman had a grip-sack full of prepared poetry with him, and a large fund of raw material under his glossy silk hat. Although he has seen 75 summers, Mr. Gay can still evolve poetry with his eyes shut, and

---

[239] This information is from Devon Heritage; online at www.devonheritage.org

[240] Bill Moore 1987. *Words That Taste Good: More Than 600 Short, Sharp, Sparkling Bits of Poetry*. Pembroke Publishers Limited.

[241] Moore 1987:100. Bill Moore 1987. *Words That Taste Good: More Than 600 Short, Sharp, Sparkling Bits of Poetry*. Pembroke Publishers Limited.

if the reader detects anything unusually poetic in the *Spectator* during coming days, it will be because of the poetic visit.

The next day, this appeared in the Guelph *Mercury & Advertiser*:

> Mr. James Gay now diversifies his occupation with the muse by playing the flute and accordeon (*sic*) on the streets.

The following quote is from an 1885 ad in *Foot-ball: its history for five centuries*:[242]

> As the brightest of poets have passed away,
> Now it's left between Tennyson and James Gay."
> Canada's Poet: By "Yours alway, James Gay"
> (Of the Royal City of Guelph, Ontario), Poet Laureate of Canada, and
> Master of all Poets. London: Field & Tuer, The Leadenhall Press,
> E.C. "As amusing as English as She is Spoke." [One Shilling.

---

The Saturday Review has treated "Canada's Poet" as the "thinnest" joke of the generation. But the fact is this amusing book is not a joke at all. The whole point of its publication is, that like "English as She is Spoke,"[243] it is a serious book, seriously written, and its author, James Gay, is serious in believing himself to be on a level with Lord Tennyson, to whom it will be observed his "poems" are affectionately dedicated.

From *Lippincott's Monthly Magazine, a Popular Journal of General Literature* (Volume 39; 1887):

> There has lately been published on the other side of the Atlantic a little book called 'Canada's Poet' (London, Field & Tuer),[244] which is the most delightful piece of unconscious humor that has appeared since 'English as She is Spoke.' The author is James Gay. He signs himself 'Poet Laureate of Canada and Master of All Poets,' and, according to an Introduction by James Millington,[245] the labored wit of which contrasts unfavorably with the spontaneity of Mr. Gay's, he was born in 1810, and is still living in Canada. No better sample of his peculiar powers could be given than the following:

---

[242] Montague Shearman and James E. Vincent, 1885, *Historical Sporting Series* No. 1. London: Field & Tuer, The Leadenhall Press, E.C. page 84. This same ad was also included in *Echoes of Memory* by Atherton Furlong, 1884, and *The Chinese painted by themselves* by Col. Tcheng-Ki-Tong (Military Attache of China at Paris), Translated from the French by James Millington, 1885, London: Field & Truer, The Leadenhall Press, E.C.

[243] Carolino, Pedro 1883. *O Novo Guia da Conversação em Portuguez e Inglez / English As She Is Spoke*. New York: Appleton & Co.

[244] Millington, James (ed.) 1884. *James Gay; Canada's Poet*. London: Field & Tuer.

[245] Very little is known of James Millington.

The brightest of Poets have passed away.
Never a one of them composed on the Elephant and the Flea,
At last it's composed by the Poet James Gay.

## THE ELEPHANT AND THE FLEA

Between those two there's a great contrast,
The elephant is slow, the flea very fast,
You can make friends with the elephant and gain his good-will,
If you have a flea in your bed you cannot lie still:
A flea is a small thing, all times in the way.
Hopping and jumping like beasts after their prey,
Oft drop inside your ears - don't think this a wonder,
You will think for a while it's loud claps of thunder:
We can make friends with all beasts ever came in our way -
No man on earth can make friends with a flea;
The elephant is a large beast, and cunning no doubt;
If you offend him, look out for his snout;
Give him tobacco, it will make him ugly and cross,
A blow from his trunk's worse than a kick from a horse;
And still they are friendly, will cause no disaster,
Beg around in shows, make money for their master:
On this noble beast, the elephant, I have no more to say;
And this little black insect will have its own way.
A flea you may flatten if you know how,
But an elephant no man can't serve so anyhow.
One thing seems wonderful to your poet, James Gay -
All beasts and little animals seem to have a cunning way;
Just like the whales at sea, they seem to know their foes,
Upsets their boats in a moment, and down they goes.

Of course, fully to enjoy the fun of this sort of thing the reader must keep in mind that the poems are written in perfect good faith, and that their author is serious in believing himself the equal of 'Dr. C.L. Alfred Tennyson,' to whom he has dedicated his book, with the delicate suggestion, 'Now Longfellow is gone there are only two of us left. There ought to be no rivalry between us two.'

James Gay responded to this review in *The Whistling Buoy* by Charles Barnard (*Lippincott's Monthly Magazine*. J.B. Lippincott Co., June, 1887):

The Book-Talk in the April number of *Lippincott's Magazine* reviewed a book of poems by James Gay, of Ontario, Canada. The Reviewer is pleased to know that his slight notice has been appreciated by the author, as the following letter will testify. As the work of a true genius, the compositor has been instructed not to tamper with any of its orthographical, rhythmic, or grammatical peculiarities, but to set up the 'copy' exactly as it was received.

Guelph, April 18th 1887

To J B Lippincott And Co Philadelphia
Gentlemen when reading your Monthly
Magazine the other day behold I fell in with
The Elephant And Flea composed by the
Master of all Poets come from where the may
You have the names of many a bright Poet as
Long since passed away not one of those could
Compose with this Little Man James Gay
My composing with theirs is on a diferant stile
All together for the good of man makes all Heavens
Smile I was Born a Poeit Thousands on earth well
Know it all through my life understand Ive don my
Duty between God and Man always ready to do him
Good as far as I can this is the true Caractor of this fore
Said Little Man no novels or fary tales with James Gay
When ever I take my pen in hand to compose Christ tells
Me what to say all my books are composed on a solid
Rock never to cause any stumbling blocks rock
Of ages clift for me its where Ive found salvation free
From the first breath of life no malice or strife never
Enterd the Heart of James Gay this if spared will
Be caried out till he is called away to that happy
Home prepaird for all mankind where nothing can decay
I was 77 on the 24 of Last March Gladstone is four
Months older then Gay Curious for me to have this
To say My Brother Long Fellow died on my birth
Day on March 24th 1882 It appears the old poets are
Passing away only two Left Lord Tinnysan and
James Gay I am From the Parish of Brattan
Clovelly Devonshire And Alfred Tinnysan is
From the Isle of White I will asshure you my
Brother Americans as a Poet with me as no site, I have

Over two thousand five hundred pages all ready
Composed and ready for the press I want to reap
Some benefits of My Beautiful Poemes before
I am called to rest Poor Robby Burns Lord Byran
William Cooper Shake Speer Tom Moor Milton
And my Brother John Gay A Devonshire Poet to
And my self to I say thousands and tens of thousands
Of Dolars will be Made by Book Publishers all over
This world after our Bodeys have returned to clay
Ive been a great traveller in my day So now I want
Published the Life and Travels of three years
In England and Iriland and the Channal Islands and
United States and Canada To some of the best Books
Ever composed in Canada or in any other parts of
This world I have composed forty versis for Her
Majestyes Jubile I should say some of the fineist
You ever did see. * * *
I have been composing more or less
Since 61[246] I can never give it up till I am called away
My Heavenly Fathers will I must obay I sit and
Compose some nights till nine and ten some times
Till eleven I genarally take my happy repose about
Nine sleep in peace with all Mankind I am a Man
Above thousands this is so every ones friend and no
Ones foe Gentlemen this is all at present I have
To say Please send me a few lines by return
Of Post I shall feal as happy as the flowers in May
Gentlemen yours Ever truly in Christ what
More can a Poet say Address James Gay
East Market Square Royal City of Guelph
                                                    Ontario
N.B. my little Poemes through your
Monthly Magazine can never be forgot
The will sell in Unitid States and in Canada
Just like Cakes when hot."[247]

---

[246] He either means 1861, when he was 51 years old, or when he was 61 years old in 1871.

[247] *Lippincott's Magazine* 1887:1043-1044

## An Address To My Fellow-Citizens Of Guelph
(Published in 1884)

My old townsmen of Guelph, I no longer repine,
In composing this poem, giving pleasure to you and all mankind;
I've been many long years with you; this you know is true;
Not one of all could ever think the regard I've had for you.
Ofttimes you have met me in the street, pleasant, good-natured, and fine;
This I found my duty, to treat my fellow mankind...

Worked hard in this town for many a year, and tried to do my best;
And, like other misfortunes, I fell away like the rest.
This we cannot account for, this far surpasses man,
It seems as if laid out for us after doing the best we can.
As we see this before us more or less each day,
We must submit to this with patience till we are called away.
We all have our misfortunes, of this we must confess;
Fighting against troubles, till we are further blest.
Let us take all things quietly,
For here we cannot stay;
Have pity, for those unfortunates who
Are falling more or less each day.
Let all look up to the Maker of Poets,
It's Him that knows the best,
And guide you safe to your spiritual homes
To take your final rest.
What a grand thing to think of! What a reconciliation!
This home is for all mankind, for every tongue and nation.
In closing this address to you, I've done the best I can
In showing all your duties towards your fellow-man.

The following appeared in the *Guelph Daily Mercury* 21 March, 1890:

> James Gay has been sick for some time. He was able to be down street today,
> and, although not strong, he looks very well for the weight of 80 years. This
> is what he says:

> He loves all on earth with no malice or strife,
> This is why he lives a happy life.

Dear Brothers and Sisters in Guelph,
Try this on in the same kind of a way
on your birthday.
My age is eighty on Friday, 21st day.
This is all at present I have to say."

## WORKS:

"Man's Future State" by James Gay, 1878.[248]

*Biographical Information and Samples of Poetry by Guelph Poet James Gay, Ca.1880-1953*. 1880.

*Christmas Carols for 1882*, 1882. Guelph [Publisher unknown].

*Poems by James Gay...written while crossing the sea in 1882*. Guelph [Publisher/Printer unknown][249]

*Canada's Poet*, 1884. London: Field & Tuer, The Leadenhall Press, E.C.

"The Elephant and the Flea," printed in Lippincott's Monthly Magazine 1887. J.B. Lippincott and Company. Pp. 695-696.

*A Collection of Various Pieces of Poetry, Chiefly Patriotic by James Gay*. McNally & Loftin, 1964.

\*\*\*

---

[248] The following item appeared in the *Daily Mercury* on 24 September, 1878: "Jas. Gay, the poet, will have for sale in a few days at the bookstores his piece on 'Man's Future State.' Mr. Gay pronounces this piece to be one of his best productions."

[249] See Appendix E.

# XXVIII

## ⒼEORGE ⒿORRISH

### 2 MARCH, 1831, DARTMOOR, DEVONSHIRE, ENGLAND - 5 JUNE, 1912, GUELPH

George Norrish was born at Dartmeet on the easterly corner of the parish of Lidford, Dartmoor, Devon, England. He came to Canada with his parents in 1843 and eventually settled in Nassagaweya, Ontario. Later, he moved to Guelph, where he ran a grocery store in the Howitt Block on Carden Street. In 1851 he married Elizabeth Easterbrook, of Brookville. For 24 years George was choir leader and organist at Ebenezer United Church.[250] The Ebenezer orchestra that accompanied the choir consisted of three Easterbrooks and George Norrish on violin. He also brought his melodeon and played "for the edification of the congregation."[251] George's brother Joshua wrote a pamphlet entitled "The Early History of Nassagaweya."[252] George is buried in the Ebenezer Cemetery in Darbyville, Halton Regional Municipality, Ontario, Canada. His headstone reads:

> George Norrish - Born at Manor of 'Blackslade', called 'Blacheslach' in the Domesday Book, Dartmeet, Devon, England, March 2, 1831...Left Plymouth on 3 master "Cosmopolite" Apr. 1843...Married Elizabeth Easterbrook Nov. 3. 1854. Choirmaster Ebenezer 30 yrs. Author, sold first Melodeons & Reapers in these parts. Died Guelph June 5, 1912.

Norrish "had the ability of putting all the activities of the community in verse form, and had a book of humorous poems published."[253] He was also a correspondent for the Guelph *Weekly Herald*. For instance, he wrote a long piece entitled "More About the Scott Act," printed in that newspaper under "Letters to the Editor" on 6 October, 1887. In the *Daily Mercury* of 5 September, 1878, the following item appeared:

---

[250] *Acton Free Press*, 13 June 1912, page 3, column 5.

[251] Online at http://www.ebenezeruc.ca/history.htm

[252] *George Norrish*. Guelph Historical Society Publications; Volume 1, Number 1 (1961). This short article incorrectly has his birth date as March 3rd, 1831.

[253] *Memoirs of George Norrish*, 1911.

Mr. Geo. Norrish, of Nassagaweya, left a large quantity of excellent eating apples for the consumption of the printers connected with the Mercury office.

## A Panegyric on the Bell Organ

'A Panegyric on the Bell Organ' by George Norrish, a Guelph poet and long time employee of the Bell Organ Company[254]:

> What is home like
> without a Bell organ?
> A prison, asylum; a jail
> Where no one will stay
> but a culprit
> Unable to find any bail

Golick has noted that, "traces of Canadian cultural expression are found in the printed poems of local amateur poets, such as C.T. Daniels,[255] James Gay, and George Norrish. 'Selling Apples in Guelph Market in the Palmy Days of 1879' by Norrish, describes Guelph as a bustling centre of commercial activity at that time. Another poem by Norrish, 'A Panegyric on the Bell Organ,' describes the large Bell organ factory with hundreds of workers and humorously suggests that a solution to troubles in Ireland was possible with the purchase of a Bell organ:

> If Ireland would take the Bell Organ,
> And learn to play God Save the Queen,
> The 'Rose' would embrace the sweet 'Shamrock,'
> And the 'Orange' would blend with the 'Green.'"[256]

---

[254] Coulman 1977:11

[255] Charles T. Daniel; see section XII.

[256] Golick 2010:19

## SELLING APPLES IN GUELPH MARKET
## IN THE PALMY DAYS OF 1879

(In George Norrish's *Poems: Humorous, Sentimental and Political* - 1888)[257]

Such a passing and repassing,
Such a hurrying to and fro;
Quite a mystery where they come from,
More a mystery where they go.
Some on duty, some on business,
Some for pleasure, some in pain;
Some for travel, with their satchel,
Hurrying up to catch the train:
Young people out for pleasure,
Hailing every chum they meet;
Pa's and Mamma's, more at leisure,
Keeping time with little feet.

Here are urchins selling papers -
Calling on the crowd to buy;
Yonder sharpers cutting capers
To deceive the human eye.
Here a clerk with down-cast features -
Just received his tailor's dun.
There's a plow-boy, happy creature,
Carrying home his new bought gun.
Ladies in the choicest satin,
Labourers in the coarsest gray.
Farmers with each other chatting
On the price of corn and hay.

---

[257] Much later, in 2002, for Guelph's 175th anniversary, James Gordon, a Guelph musician/politician, set this to music (James Gordon: "Song of Our City; A Musical Celebration of Guelph." Pipe Street Records. Manifest Productions - Produced by James Gordon for Guelph Museums 2002 (CD).

Omnibuses, hurrying onward,
With their loads of human freight.
Spooney young men, asking maidens,
If they're coming out tonight.
Coming out from post office,
Tearing envelopes like mad,
Find perhaps some darling's photo
Or a scolding from their dad.

Perhaps a line from some poor debtor,
Asking time for money due;
Or what's worse, a lawyer's letter
Telling him he's going to sue.
Auctioneers with crowds around them,
Selling goods at half their cost,
Yet the artful rogues (confound them),
All get rich by what they've lost.
Butcher's carts with lots of mutton,
Baker's vans with loaves of bread,
Policemen, with great brass buttons,
Measured step and stately tread.

Farmer, merchants, huxters, butchers,
Fain would sell to all they meet,
All commingle, hustle, bustle,
Up and down our Wyndham street
All purambulating onward,
Upward, downward, there and back,
Unless you're willing to be trod on,
You had better clear the track.

Apples! see those boys (confound them!)
Where on earth are the police?
Butcher! catch those boys and hold them,
There they go with two apiece!
Apples, man! just take and try them,
It isn't rot, it's just a speck,
They're excellent, and if you'll buy them,
I'll sell them at ten cents a peck.

**135**

**WORKS:**

George Norrish: *Poems: Humorous, Sentimental and Political* (Guelph, Herald Office; 1888, 85 pages).[258]

\*\*\*

---

[258] Golick (2010) has this publication dated to 1891, but in the *Herald* Table of Golick's thesis, it is dated as 1888.

# XXIX

## "Ricardo"

### Flourished 1887-1892

The identity of "Ricardo," probably a pseudonym for either a male or female versifier, remains unknown. This versifier also wrote an occasional column for the Guelph *Weekly Herald*, for instance a short piece entitled "Ricardo's Reflections" (6 October, 1887).

### [FRAGMENT: Title unknown]
("Guelph, Feb. 4th, '92"; Printed in *The Herald*)

...every movement for the city...

He loved his country - loved her as a son;
    He loved his party, and through each campaign
    With real untiring worked with might and main;
Yet 'twas the love of country spurred him on.

And now that his great heart has ceased to beat
    And Grit and Tory clasp hands o'er his bier,
    In unison they'll shed a silent tear,
And bury thoughts of victory or defeat.

The bells ring forth their sadly solemn knell;
    And loving hearts are plunged in bitter grief,
    And widespread sympathy brings no relief -
But ministering Angels whisper: "It is well."

\*\*\*

# XXX

## 𝕵ames 𝕸cIntyre

BAPTISED 25 MAY, FORRES, SCOTLAND -
31 MARCH, 1906, INGERSOLL, ONTARIO, CANADA

James McIntyre, labeled the "Cheese Poet," after his "Dairy and Cheese Odes," had several verses printed in the *Toronto Globe* "as comic relief."[259] He was later (1927) celebrated in Deacon's *The Four Jameses*.[260] Although McIntyre demonstrated a "lack of literary skills,"[261] he was popular and has a long-lasting legacy of an annual poetry contest held in his honor at Ingersoll, Ontario, "sponsored by The Ingersoll Times and the Corporation of the Town of Ingersoll."[262]

### GALT AND DUNLOP
(Published in 1884)[263]

Galt and Doctor Dunlop witty
They located and planned the city
Of Guelph, and they cut the first tree down,
The stump was the centre of the town.

From thence the streets radiate like fan,
And they project on this same plan
The towns of Stratford and Goderich,
The last it stands near broad Huron's beach,

---

[259] See the Wikipedia article on James McIntyre (poet).

[260] His poem "Galt and Dunlop" also appears in Hugh Douglass' 1963 notebook entitled "Poems by local writers in the early Guelph Newspapers (unpublished manuscript in the Guelph Public Library, Rare Books Archive).

[261] Ibid.

[262] Ibid.

[263] McIntyre 1884:60-61. Noted in Douglass 1963.

Conspicuous on a bluff so grand,
'Neath which doth flow the clear Maitland,
Of glorious view you may partake,
Gazing on Huron's mighty lake.

**WORKS:**

James McIntyre 1884. *Musings on the Banks of the Canadian River Thames*. Ingersoll: H. Rowland, *Tribune* Printing Press.

James McIntyre 1889. *Poems of James McIntyre*.

\* \* \*

# XXXI

## 𝔇. 𝔍. 𝔍.

### FLOURISHED 1892

The identity of D.F.F. remains unknown. Thomas Goldie was elected Mayor of Guelph in 1891. He was related to James Goldie, who enlarged the mill now known as Goldie Mill in 1867, on the Speed River; 75 Cardigan Street.

### THOMAS GOLDIE ESQUIRE
("Guelph, February 6th, 1892" Printed in *The Herald* 8 February, 1892)

Why all this mourning; those flags lowly
    waving,
Why gather such crowds on the corners
    to-day?
Read the sad look on each face, it will an-
    swer,
The city's true friend has been taken away.

Knowing his worth for whatever he labored,
The highest the city could grant him it
    gave,
And proudly it looked on its great-hearted
    Chieftain,
But soon he'll be sleeping alone in his
    grave.

Ah! well may the people in sorrow now
    gather,
To pay a last tribute to one they held dear;
Full many a heart he made happier and
    lighter,
For he was endowed with affection sincere.

While calmly he'll sleep in the graveyard so
    silent,
He will live in the mem'ry of all he had
    known,
Till the last summons calling in rapture
    will bring them,
To share that bright home where his spirit
    has flown.

\*\*\*

# XXXII

## 𝕷𝕿. 𝕮ol. 𝕵ohn 𝕸cCrae MD

**30 November, 1872, Guelph -**
**28, January, 1918, Boulogne, France**
**Buried in Wimereux Cemetery, France**

Lieutenant-Colonel John McCrae was born in Guelph, Ontario to Lieutenant-Colonel David McCrae and Janet Simpson Eckford. Comprehensive biographies of Guelph's most famous versifier can easily be found elsewhere.[264] However, the present collection offers a fresh opportunity to reassess the poetic Guelph context which, in some measure, contributed as a potential influence upon John McCrae's writings. We have already seen[265] how his father, David, was overseer to John Inglis at McCrae & Armstong's woollen manufactory, during that poet's residency in Guelph from 1872-1874. It is therefore intriguing that the Inglis poem "Ode To Peace" includes the line:

"The fair fields of earth thou hast deluged in blood."[266]

John McCrae would only have been a baby when the Scottish weaver poet was in town, but even by 1914 Inglis was remembered by Guelph friends, and it is not impossible his poetry had a place in the McCrae household. Additionally, one of the poems in Hetty Hazelwood's[267] 1871 poetry book *A Garland Gathered At Morn*, is "Scarlet Poppies,"[268] the title alone reminding us of John McCrae's later "In Flanders Fields."

---

[264] See Further Reading, namely Prescott (1985).

[265] section XVII

[266] Inglis 1907:106-107

[267] See section XIII

[268] Hazelwood 1871:21

## A Song of Comfort
(1894)

"Sleep, weary ones, while ye may-
  Sleep, oh, sleep!"
Eugene Field

Thro' May time blossoms, with whisper low,
  The soft wind sang to the dead below:
"Think not with regret on the Springtime's song
  And the task ye left while your hands were strong.
The song would have ceased when the Spring was past,
  And the task that was joyous be weary at last."

To the winter sky when the nights were long
  The tree-tops tossed with a ceaseless song:
"Do ye think with regret on the sunny days
  And the path ye left, with its untrod ways?
The sun might sink in a storm cloud's frown
  And the path grow rough when the night came down."

In the grey twilight of the autumn eves,
  It sighed as it sang through the dying leaves:
"Ye think with regret that the world was bright,
  That your path was short and your task was light;
The path, though short, was perhaps the best
  And the toil was sweet, that it led to rest."[269]

---

[269] McCrae 1919:38-39

## UNSOLVED
(1895)

Amid my books I lived the hurrying years,
    Disdaining kinship with my fellow man;
Alike to me were human smiles and tears,
    I cared not whither Earth's great life-stream ran,
Till as I knelt before my mouldered shrine,
    God made me look into a woman's eyes;
And I, who thought all earthly wisdom mine,
    Knew in a moment that the eternal skies
Were measured but in inches, to the quest
    That lay before me in that mystic gaze.
"Surely I have been errant: it is best
    That I should tread, with men their human
        ways."
God took the teacher, ere the task was learned,
And to my lonely books again I turned.[270]

## ANARCHY
(1897)

I saw a city filled with lust and shame,
    Where men, like wolves, slunk through the grim half-light;
And sudden, in the midst of it, there came
    One who spoke boldly for the cause of Right.

And speaking, fell before that brutish race
    Like some poor wren that shrieking eagles tear,
While brute Dishonour, with her bloodless face
    Stood by and smote his lips that moved in prayer.

"Speak not of God! In centuries that word
    Hath not been uttered! Our own king are we."
And God stretched forth his finger as He heard
    And o'er it cast a thousand leagues of sea.[271]

---

[270] McCrae 1919:18

[271] McCrae 1919:28

## DISARMAMENT
(1899)

One spake amid the nations, "Let us cease
From darkening with strife the fair
World's light,
We who are great in war be great in peace.
No longer let us plead the cause by might."

But from a million British graves took birth
A silent voice - the million spake as one -
"If ye have righted all the wrongs of earth
Lay by the sword! Its work and ours is done."[272]

**WORKS:**

Lt. Col. John McCrae 1919. *In Flanders Fields and other poems, with An Essay in Character by Sir Andrew Macphail.* Toronto: William Briggs.

\*\*\*

---

[272] McCrae 1919:29

1879 Advertisement for Guelph *Daily Mercury* Printing.

# Appendix A

## Guelph Newspapers

---

## Guelph Newspapers

The following chronological outline of 19th century Guelph newspapers is a synthesis of several sources[273] and an informative short essay by William H. Cooper (29 June, 1987) which appears at the beginning of the first microfilm in the Guelph Public Library archives for *The Herald* (1842):[274]

### THE HERALD *I*
(1842: ran for nine months)
"The first newspaper in Guelph was the first version of the *Guelph Herald*. The first issue of the first version was published 15 January 1842. The paper's publisher was Charles H. McDonnell.[275] Its actual owner was Henry William Peterson. It lasted for nine months, for McDonnell moved to Rochester, N.Y."[276]

### THE WELLINGTONIAN
(c.1842/3: ran for only a few weeks)[277]
"The *Wellingtonian*, followed it [the first *Herald*] after six months in 1843. Also destined to be short-lived, it had as its publisher and editor one Willett."[278]

---

[273] Burrows 1877; Stead 2002; original Guelph Directories and newspaper archives.

[274] Guelph Public Library microfilm archives.

[275] Charles Macdonald according to Burrows (1877: 58), or Charles McDonnell according to Stead (2002:13). The *Herald* of 19 February, 1842 names him as Chas. H. M'Donnell.

[276] Cooper 1987

[277] Burrows 1877:58

[278] Cooper 1987

## THE ADVERTISER
(1844-1873)

The *Guelph Advertiser* "was established by John Smith[279] in 1844. Originally called the *Guelph & Galt Advertiser*, it continued under Smith who was Guelph's first mayor in 1856[280] (see section VI), until the latter's defeat at the polls in 1857. A tri-weekly version of the paper was published between roughly 1854 and 1861. The Rev. Peter Clerihew bought the paper that year [1861], late of the Berlin *Telegraph*,[281] and soon sold it to the Hon. Adam Johnston Fergusson Blair, the local member of Parliament for Wellington South who was later in the Dominion cabinet under Sir John A. Macdonald as President of the Privy Council until his death in December 1867. In 1858, Blair sold the paper to Jonathan Wilkinson, who turned it 'into a daily, amalgamating with the *Mercury* in 1873.'[282] With this merge, the paper was, for a time, called the *Mercury and Advertiser*. 'Judging from the *Advertiser*'s subtitle for a period, it also had circulation in Elora and Fergus.'"[283]
Office (1873): "St. George's Square, near the Montreal Bank."[284]

## THE HERALD *II*
(1847-1924)

"The next paper to appear was the second version of the *Guelph Herald* in June 1847, which was founded as a weekly by F.D. Austin, joined soon by one Pearson.[285] George Pirie (see section V above), Col. James Webster and H.W. Peterson in 1848 formed a joint stock company, with the first mentioned [George Pirie] being made editor of this paper."[286] The full title of the newspaper, in the period 1847-8, was *The Guelph Herald and Literary, Agricultural and Commercial Gazette*. Daily poems on the front page and a poetry section were regularly included. George Pirie "was to remain editor until his death in 1870, in the meanwhile also publishing the *Fergus Freeholder* (founded 19 August 1854)."[287] The *Herald* was conducted by George Pirie's widow until December 1871.[288] "From 1870 the

---

[279] Burrows 1877:57

[280] Stead 2002:13

[281] Burrows 1877:97. There exist archives of an 1857 *Clerihew's Weekly Journal* at the Guelph Public Library (Main Branch).

[282] The 1873 Guelph Directory lists only Joseph H. Hacking as the publisher and proprietor of the *Advertiser*, presumably immediately after it amalgamated with the *Mercury*.

[283] Cooper 1987

[284] 1873 Guelph Directory.

[285] It remains unknown whether this was John Pearson (see section XI).

[286] Cooper 1987

[287] Cooper 1987

[288] Burrows 1877:150

editor of the Herald was George Pirie's son Alex P. Pirie [*sic*: Alexander Fraser Pirie (1849-1903)[289]]. In 1871 Frederick J. Chadwick[290] purchased the paper...Meanwhile a daily edition appeared. In 1877 C. Acton Burrows became a partner, but sold out his interest in 1878 to Smallpiece. In 1881 Smallpiece became the sole owner. In 1882 Chadwick again became the proprietor. In 1885 Smallpiece sold his interest to Henry Gummer...The Guelph Herald Limited having been formed, Henry Gummer remained proprietor of the paper until it was absorbed by the *Mercury* in its daily edition 31 December 1923 and in its weekly edition on 3 January 1924. From the time of George Pirie at least, this paper remained Conservative in political slant."[291]

"It's fearless advocacy of the Conservative party, and the unflinching opposition it offered to everything savoring of meaness (*sic*) or trickery in local or general politics, as well as the ability displayed in its editorial columns, and the enterprise shown in the news department, stamping it from the commencement as a high class newspaper, destined to exert a powerful influence on the future of the District, a mission which it most emphatically accomplished."[292]

Office (1873): "Garden Street, adjoining Queen's Hotel."[293]

## WELLINGTON OR WEEKLY MERCURY (1853)
## THE MERCURY (1853/4-1867)
## THE GUELPH DAILY MERCURY (1867-present)

After the second *Herald*, the next paper to appear at Guelph turned out to be the most long-lived.[294] This paper commenced as the *Wellington* or *Weekly Mercury* in September 1853 under George M. Keeling until his death in October 1861. While Cooper states that George Palmer succeeded Keeling as editor, Burrows stated that in 1861 Keeling died and the *Mercury* was taken over by John Keller.[295] In 1862 James Innes became the publisher and proprietor.[296] The publisher was Robert M. Longan. James Innes and John C. McLagan became joint proprietors shortly afterwards, situated at "#10 Day's Block, di-

---

[289] Alexander Fraser Pirie was a Canadian journalist and newspaper editor, beginning his career in 1849 with his father at the Guelph *Herald*. A full article on A.F. Pirie can be found online in Wikipedia.

[290] Frederick Jasper Chadwick, an alderman who was elected mayor of Guelph in 1877 (Stead 2002:13).

[291] Cooper 1987

[292] Burrows 1877:58

[293] 1873 Guelph Directory. When The *Herald* was published by Henry Gummer, it is described as 'located in the Douglas Street building that today bears his name' (Stead 2002:13).

[294] Cooper 1987. *The Guelph Daily Mercury* continues, but now (2014) published by Grand River Media, a division of the Metroland Media Group Ltd., a subsidiary of the Torstar Corporation. For the history of the *Guelph Tribune* (1987-present), see the appropriate article on Wikipedia.

[295] Burrows 1877:122

[296] Stead 2002:13; 1873 Guelph Directory.

rectly opposite the Market."[297] They began the daily edition of the Mercury in 1867. McLagan retired in 1869 (later to travel west and establish the *Vancouver World* - 1888). By 1873, there was also an *Evening Mercury*, the offices situated on "Macdonnell Street, east of Wyndham."[298] Innes continued as sole proprietor of the *Mercury* until 1874, when John A. Davidson was included as a partner. On 1 August 1898, Innes and Davidson sold the *Mercury* to James Innes McIntosh - Mr. Innes' nephew - and Frank W. Galbraith.[299]

One of the most influential Guelph newspapermen in the 19th century was James Innes who took on a partner, John Davidson, in 1894. Innes controlled the paper for 36 years, including the fourteen year period when he served as Guelph's Liberal Member of Parliament (1882-96). "The *Mercury* recruited talented writers and editors over the years, including novelist and historian Thomas B. Costain,[300] who worked as an editor at the *Mercury* before going on to a career in the United States as associated editor of the *Saturday Evening Post* and the author of *The Black Rose* and *Son of a Hundred Kings*."[301]

Like the *Herald*, the *Mercury* regularly featured poems on its front page and in a dedicated poetry section. In the *Daily Mercury* of 1893, the following anonymous poem appeared:

## MERCURY CARRIER BOY'S ADDRESS
(Printed 23 December, 1893)

Good people, please take notice, that your Carrier is here
To verify the calendar and punctuate the year;
For the sun might be delinquent, and the moon forget to sail,
And the New Year be behind hand, but the Carrier cannot fail.

In all weathers and all seasons, though the sky were gray or blue,
He has circled in his orbit till he came around to you;
Like the planets in their courses he has kept upon his way,
And is now in perihelion, make a note of that today.

Like the common things of life that are not valued until missed,
Like the sunlight, well, just fancy, if it left the hills unkissed!
Like your daily bread and butter, which you could not do without,
Is the matutinal visitor that brings the news about.

---

[297] 1864 ad in the *Mercury*.

[298] 1873 Guelph Directory.

[299] Cooper 1987

[300] A full treatment on Thomas B. Costain is available on Wikipedia.

[301] Stead 2002:13

Kings and princes of an older time, the conquerors of the earth,
Had no fair appreciation of the interviewer's worth;
The benighted chap of old, the ancient hero, poet, scholar,
Never knew the chaste delight of tipping Carrier's half-a-dollar.

Even Adam in the garden, in a perfect state of bliss,
Had no paper with his breakfast, oh, ye growlers, think of this!
Alexander, cutting capers with the kingdoms fast and loose,
Throned and sceptered, had to put up with the stalest kind of news.

Uncle Solomon, the Wise Man, had to fold his hands and wait
For a line from Mrs. Sheba, or from Babylon the Great:
And in Rome, the superb city, while the flames rose higher and higher,
Nero couldn't buy an extra with the latest from the fire.

But the century has clothed you with conveniences to date,
Such as shame the ancient monarchs with their rude imperial state;
Newspapers being not the least of luxuries today,
And the Carrier - ah, the **MERCURY** Carrier! remember him I pray.

### THE GUELPH CHRONICLE
#### (1867-1868)
In 1866, John Smith (see section VI), previously establishing the *Advertiser*, from which he had departed in 1857, purchased the *Oil Springs Chronicle*, (the latter founded in 1861 - Oil Springs was later to be called Petrolea). This paper moved to Guelph in 1867 and re-named the *Guelph Chronicle*. It was absorbed by the *Elora Observer*, 14 February 1868.[302]

### THE ECHO
#### (1877)
The *Echo* briefly appeared in 1877.[303]

### THE SATURDAY SUN
#### (1888-1889)
The *Saturday Sun* was published by James Hough Jr. during 1888-89.[304]

---

[302] Cooper 1987

[303] Cooper 1987

[304] Cooper 1987

### THE GUELPH ADVOCATE (1896-1900)
### TWICE-A-WEEK ADVOCATE (1897-1900)

When *The Advocate* was established in the 1890's, the citizens of Guelph were served by three daily newspapers. The *Guelph Advocate* appeared in a daily edition in 1896, with a semi-weekly called the *Twice-A-Week Advocate* appearing in 1897. The paper lasted until December 1900. The Guelph Advocate Printing Company was the proprietor of this paper, and was politically independent.[305]

\* \* \*

---

[305] Cooper 1987

# 𝔄ppendix 𝔅

## Guelph 19th Century Bookstores

---

### J. Leggett
1852: "Books, Stationery, Berlin Wool, and Fancy Goods."[306]

### Shewan's Bookstore
1866: "Wyndham Street opposite the English Church"[307]
[St. George's church when it was in the centre of St. George's Square].

### Thornton's
1869: "Bookstore and Binders - Near the Post Office."[308]

### Cuthbert's Bookstore
Proprietor: Robert Cuthbert
1869: Wyndham Street[309]

### John Anderson
1873: East side Wyndham Street.[310]

---

[306] 23 December, 1852 *Advertiser* advertisement.

[307] 21 October, 1866 *Mercury* advertisement.

[308] Ad printed in the *Evening Mercury* on 20 April, 1869.

[309] See Appendix C for Cuthbert's Circulating Library and promotional acrostic poem.

[310] 1873 Guelph Directory.

## T.J. Day

Established 1862
1862-1872: 'opposite the Market'[311]
1872-after 1878: West side Wyndham Street.[312]
1894: 29 Wyndham Street.


## C.F. Pashley

1873: Day's Block, Lower Wyndham Street.[313]


## Petrie's Bookstore

Proprietor: Robert W. Petrie, then, as of 1893 Elizabeth Petrie
1880: "Masonic Hall Block, Guelph."[314]
1892: 113 Wyndham Street.


## The City Bookstore

Proprietor: J.A. Nelles, then C.L. Nelles
1879: 24 Wyndham Street[315]
1887: "Our store is in Cutten's Block, and is known as the Arcade."[316]
1894: St. George's Square

## John Smith

Proprietor: John Smith (1894)
1894: 20 Wyndham Street.

\*\*\*

---

[311] The *Herald* supplementary edition of 1878.

[312] 1873 Guelph Directory.

[313] *Ibid*.

[314] Ad in the *Daily Mercury* on 24 January, 1880. Robert W. Petrie was a relative of Guelph druggist Alexander Bain (A.B.) Petrie. Robert died in 1893 and the Bookstore was run by his widow Elizabeth. Thanks to Shannon Christie, great great grand-daughter of A.B. Petrie, for these genealogical details.

[315] *Mercury* advertisement 14 May, 1879.

[316] 6 October, 1887 *Herald* advertisement.

# Appendix C

## Guelph Printers and Book Binders

---

### The Guelph Advertiser Printing Office
(1847)

John Smith - Proprietor

"The Publisher of the *Guelph Advertiser* having made additions to his Printing Office, from the **Buffalo Type Foundry**, and being in expectation of a variety of FANCY TYPE from **England**, by the first ships, flatters himself that he will be able to execute EVERY VARIETY OF PRINTING, In a style equal to any office in Western Canada, and at reasonable prices."[317]

### G. M. Keeling
(1853)

"Church Street, Guelph, near the post office."[318]

### The Herald Book and Job Establishment
(1864)

Wyndham Street.

---

[317] Ad printed in the *Guelph & Galt Advertiser*, 27 August, 1847.

[318] Ad printed in the *Advertiser* 6 January, 1853.

## THORNTON'S

(1869)

"Bookstore and Binders - Near the Post Office."[319]

The proprietor, signing simply as "C."[320] penned the following promotional acrostic poem that appeared in the *Evening Mercury* 21 March, 1869:

**T**he e's a power whose magic spell
**H**as made the heart with rapture swell,
**O**r caused it oft to throb with pain,
**R**eflected from the human brain.
**N**ow name to me this potent power,
**T**hat rules the monarch of the hour;
**O** yes, I can, for on this page,
**N**ow sullied o'er with dust and age,
**S**weet memories rise from out the past.

**B**lurr'd with tears - aye falling fast,
**O**n ev'ry word there written now,
**O**r sentence too, there breathes a vow,
**K**eeps sacred shall this souvenir.

**S**tay e'er with me, I hold so dear,
**T**hus by the power of ink and pen,
**O**f those we ne'er shall meet again;
**R**emain their thoughts - the same in print,
**E**nvolved from every thinking mint.


## THE MERCURY STEAM PRINTING HOUSE

(1869)

"McLagan & Innes - Mercury Office, Guelph"[321]

---

[319] Ad printed in the *Evening Mercury* on 20 April, 1869.

[320] See Appendix H.

[321] Ad in the *Evening Mercury* 9 March, 1869.

## FARMERS' AND MECHANICS' INSTITUTE OF GUELPH
(1870)[322]

## THE GUELPH BOOKBINDERY
(1873)

"Guelph Bookbindery, St. George's Square, Next door to the Advertiser Office. All kinds of Books and Magazines neatly bound. Blank Books made to order. Ruling done to any pattern. Robert Easton, Proprietor."[323]

## HACKING'S EXCELSIOR PRINTING HOUSE
(1874)

Joseph H. Hacking - Proprietor

James Patterson - Foreman

"Plain and Fancy Book & Job Printing. First Prize winner at the Guelph Central Exhibition in 1874 and 1875 for the best specimens of ornamental and letterpress work. At the corner of Wyndham Street and St. George's Square."[324]

## T. CHAPMAN, BOOKBINDER
(1875/6/7)

"At 42 Wyndham Street."

## THE HERALD STEAM PRINTING HOUSE
(1877)

"The Herald Steam Printing House

Is one of the most replete in the Dominion, containing all the latest styles of type, the most modern machinery, and in which none but first-class workmen are employed, thus ensuring to the public the execution of their work in a manner that cannot be excelled and at moderate prices. All orders executed with dispatch and punctuality. Samples and estimates sent to any address."[325]

## KELSO & GROFF
### - SUCCESSORS TO J.H. HACKING -
(1879)

"Book and Job printers, Bond's Block,
corner of Wyndham street and St. George's Square, Guelph."

---

[322] See Appendix D below.

[323] Ad in the 1873 Guelph Directory.

[324] Ad in the 1875/6/7 Guelph Directory.

[325] Ad at the end of Burrows 1877.

## O. E. TURNBULL, PRINTER AND BINDER
(1879)

## NUNAN BOOKBINDERY
(1880)
Proprietor: Frank Nunan[326]
"Bookbinder and Blank Book Manufacturer."[327]
1880: 81 Upper Wyndham Street
1894: 83 Wyndham Street

## WORLD PUBLISHING COMPANY
(1889)
Proprietor: J.W. Lyon
"Subscription Book Publishers
Douglas [street] one door north of post office."[328]

## KELSO'S PRINTING OFFICE
(1894)
St. George's Square (Tovell's Block).

## JAMES HOUGH BOOKBINDING
(1894)
Market Square.

## MERCURY ELECTRIC PRESS
(1895)

## MERCURY BOOK AND JOB PRESS
(1899)

\*\*\*

---

[326] See Golick 2010.

[327] Ad in the 1892/94 Guelph Directory.

[328] Ad in the 1889 Guelph Directory.

# Appendix D

## Guelph Libraries

---

### Sandilands' Circulating Library
(1832-?)

Thomas Sandilands built his home and store on the east side of Wyndham Street, between Carden and Macdonell streets (later known as the Macdonald-Love Block) in 1832, and "at the rear maintained a circulating library, Guelph's first library."[329]

### The Farmers' and Mechanics' Institute Library
(1850-1883)

The Farmers' and Mechanics' Institute was established in 1850 and operated from rooms in City Hall. Charles Julius Mickle (see Appendix E), son of the poet William Julius Mickle, served as the first president of the Institute. He also maintained a comprehensive personal library at his home "Forrest Hill" on the Elora Road (north of what is now Woodlawn Road).[330]

### R. Cuthbert's Circulating Library
(Flourished 1869)

"The Subscriber has pleasure in announcing the establishment of a Library for public circulation. This is a want that is very much needed in Guelph, and from the conviction that it will be an advantage to the public - one which will be felt and appreciated - its institution is undertaken."[331] An ad in the *Evening Mercury* (10 March, 1869) proclaims "Educate, Educate - It is the Panacea for every Social Evil. Subscribe to Cuthbert's Circulating Library, only $1 per year in advance. Cuthbert's Bookstore, Wyndham Street, Guelph."

---

[329] Durtnell 1987:35.

[330] Crowley 1987. See the Further Reading section.

[331] Ad entitled "Prospectus of Cuthbert's Circulating Library" in the *Evening Mercury* 29 January, 1869.

## Mrs Winstanley's Lending Library
(Flourished 1872)

This short-lived lending library was operated by Elizabeth Winstanley (born 1837 in Scotland) in 1872 from Upper Wyndham Street ("Next door to Mr. Naismith's").[332] Elizabeth is described as a dressmaker in the 1871 Census. Her husband was the Guelph Barrister-at-Law, Israel Winstanley.[333] They lived on Arthur Street (Guelph) from 1867.

## Guelph Public Library
(1883-1905)
(Carnegie Library: 1905-1964)

Ontario's first public library opened in Guelph on 9 February, 1883. The Mechanic's Institute library collection, housed in the old City Hall, was transferred to the new library. An attractive Neoclassical domed structure was partially funded by the Scottish-American industrialist and philanthropist, Andrew Carnegie (1835-1919), and existed from 1905 to 1964, when it was demolished - a decision that still reverberates annoyance through heritage-minded Guelphites.

\* \* \*

---

[332] Advertisement in the *Mercury* on 17 July, 1872; the ad is dated 27 May, 1872.

[333] It is interesting to note that, in 1687, William Winstanley wrote *The Lives of the Most Famous English Poets*. It is not known if there is any family connection with the later Winstanley family of Guelph.

# Appendix E

## Books Published in Guelph 1827-1899

Charles T. Daniel 1864. *William and Annie: or, A Tale of Love and War and Other Poems.*
  Guelph: Printed at the "Herald" Book and Job Establishment, Wyndham Street.

William Kingsmill 1864. *The Greenwood Tragedy: Three Addresses Delivered to the Prisoners in Toronto Gaol, Soon After the Suicide of William Greenwood, and Having Reference to that Event, to Which is Added an Appeal to the Ladies of Canada.*
  Guelph: Printed at the "Herald" Book and Job Office.[334]

William Kingsmill 1869. *Story of the Old Marine!*
  Guelph: Printed at the "Herald" office.

William E. Bessey 1870. *Evidence of Ancient Civilization in America Constituting a Lecture Delivered on Behalf of the Mechanics' Institute on Tuesday, 1st of March, 1870.*
  Guelph: Mechanics' Institute of Guelph 1870.

Willis J. Powell and John Solomon Rarey 1874. *Tachyhippodamia or, The new secret of taming horses.*
  Guelph: Megaffin.

George Pirie 1874. *Lyrics By The Late George Pirie, Esq., For Twenty-Two Years Editor and Proprietor of the Guelph Herald.*
  Guelph: Printed at the Herald Book and Job Printing Establishment.

Charles Acton Burrows 1877. *The Annals of the Town of Guelph, 1827-1877.*
  Guelph: Herald Steam Printing House.

Robert Thompson 1877. *A Brief Sketch of the Early History of Guelph.*
  Guelph: Mercury Steam Printing.

A.E.L. Treleaven 1877. *Guelph's Fiftieth Anniversary: A Poem.*
  Guelph: Herald Steam Printing Establishment.

---

[334] A photocopy of this speech is held in the rare books archive at the Guelph Public Library.

Mary Leslie (writing as James Thomas Jones) 1878. *The Cromaboo Mail Carrier: A Canadian Love Story*.
    Guelph: Jos. H. Hacking, Printer, St. George's Square.[335]

Thomas Laidlaw 1879. *The Old Concession Road*.
    Guelph: O. E. Turnbull, Printer and Binder.

James Gay 1882. *Christmas Carols for 1882*.
    Guelph [Publisher/Printer unknown].

James Gay 1883. *Poems by James Gay...written while crossing the sea in 1882*.
    Guelph [Publisher/Printer unknown].[336]

George Norrish 1888. *Poems: Humorous, Sentimental and Political*.
    Guelph: Herald Office.

Elizabeth Petrie 1893. *Unwritten History of Guelph*.
    Guelph: Elizabeth Petrie (Petrie's Bookstore).[337]

Alpheus Edward Byerly 1894. *The Beginning of Things in Wellington and Waterloo Counties: With Particular Reference to Guelph, Galt and Kitchener*.
    Guelph: Guelph Publishing Company, 1935.

Thomas Laidlaw 1895. *Sprigs O' Heather for Scottish Gatherings*.
    Guelph: Mercury Electric Press.

Thomas Laidlaw 1899. *The Old Concession Road*.
    Guelph: Mercury Book and Job Press.

* * *

---

[335] In her preface to this, Leslie promises a new novel, *The Gibbeline Flower Seller*, apparently never finished or published.

[336] According to Deacon's 1927 research notes for *The Four Jameses* (See Further Reading), a sole surviving typescript facsimile of this work is dated 1927-8. See the entry for James Gay in the *Dictionary of Canadian Biography*.

[337] There are advertisements for this rare book in the *Daily Mercury* (18 and 19 December, 1893; 10 January, 1894) designed as a Christmas present: "containing 24 sheets of beautiful tinted paper and 24 envelopes to match," presumably a book of 24 detachable cards with images of historic Guelph. The importance of this little book is that it means Elizabeth Petrie was the first female Guelph publisher.

# 𝔄ppendix 𝔍

## ℭharles 𝔍ulius 𝔐ickle,
## SON OF THE POET 𝔚illiam 𝔍ulius 𝔐ickle

---

The following item appeared in the Poetry Section of the Guelph *Herald* on 24 September, 1850:

"There is no Scotsman, 'frae Maidenkirk to John o' Groat's,' to whom Mickle's 'Nae luck aboot the house,' one of the most heart-affecting pictures of domestic love ever penned, is not as a household word; nor are there many Scotchmen or the descendants of such in other lands, by whom it is unknown or unappreciated [.] It may not, however, be of equal notoriety to our readers, that the only son of the talented author, (C. J. Mickle, Esq, the zealous promoter of every good work,) has been for many years President of the Guelph Total Abstinence Society, helping onward with heart and hand that great moral reformation. At the opening of the New Temperance Hall here the other evening, the following stanzas were sung by the Choir, in compliment to the venerable President of the Society, who occupied the Chair on the occasion, -Ed, *Herald* [George Pirie]." Printed under this is "Nae Luck Aboot The House (Cold Water Edition)."

William Julius Mickle (1734-1788) married Mary Tomkins in 1781 and they settled in Wheatley, Oxfordshire. He died in his fifty-fifth year, in 1788, and is buried in Forest Hill churchyard. It is noted that he "left one son, for whose benefit a collection of his father's poems was published by subscription, in one volume quarto"[338].

Charles Julius Mickle was born before 1788 and was residing in Guelph, and by 1850, at least 62 years old, was described above as "for many years President of the Guelph Total Abstinence Society." In this capacity, Mickle was noted in the Guelph *Herald*, on 3 August, 1850, as advocating "the great principle of Total Abstinence."

\*\*\*

---

[338] Lives of Scottish Poets, *The Society of Ancient Scots Re-Established A.D. 1770*. London; 1821-1822, page 121. Also see (Further Reading) Crowley 1987 and Sadek 1987 for a comprehensive treatment of Charles Julius Mickle.

# ᴀᴘᴘᴇɴᴅɪx 6

## Aɴ Aɴᴏɴʏᴍᴏᴜꜱ Vᴇʀꜱɪꜰɪᴇʀ

### ᴀɴᴅ ᴀ

## Rᴇꜱᴘᴏɴꜱᴇ ꜰʀᴏᴍ Aʙᴇʀꜰᴏʏʟᴇ
## 1853

---

The following verse appeared in the *Guelph Advertiser* on 8 December, 1853. The male versifier is not named.

### Tʜᴇ Fʟᴏᴡᴇʀ ᴏꜰ Eʀᴀᴍᴏꜱᴀ
(Printed in the *Guelph Advertiser* 8 December, 1853)

There is a flower in Eramosa,
As fair as e'er could flourish;
As fair as a fond father could
Or tender mother nourish,

Guelph need not talk of handsome girls,
Puslinch, nor Waterloo;
For if they've any half so fair,
I'm sure they're precious few.

Her hair is brown, her eyes are blue,
Her brow most nobly seem,
Her cheeks and lips like strawberries
When smother'd up in cream.

Her smile is more delicious than
The fragrant Scottish rose,
Yes, lovelier than the lily fair
That in the garden grows.

Her beauty, O ye Gods! cannot
In common words be told;
For her I'd face a raging main,
Or meet a lion bold.

Of her perfections 'tis in vain
For one like me to write,
Excuse me then true lovers all
When you these lines recite.

Was the great Lord Byron living,
And of this maiden hear,
He'd sound her praises, singing
Melodiously and clear.

I'm sorry friends I dare not tell
Where doth this fair one live, -
She's got my heart, I own she has,
That's all that I can give.

You may know me, I'm young and stout,
Just coming in my prime, -
She's got me fast bound in her chains,
Condemned without a crime.

If I this fair one's heart could win,
And in wedlock's bonds be tied,
In Eramosa then I'd dwell
And ever more reside.

But if her heart I do not win,
To foreign lands I'll steer;
I'll bid farewell to all my friends
Before another year.

[At the earnest request of the love-sick swain, we publish the foregoing sentimental effusion; hoping that this public expression of his sentiments may soften the heart of the fair one, and so favor his suit as to retain his *valuable* presence and *fine* poetical talent amongst us. Don't we pity him.]

Eleven days later (19 December, 1853), a poem entitled "The Fairest Flower," by "Vide et Crede,"[339] was written from Aberfoyle and printed in the *Guelph Advertiser* on 22 December:

## THE FAIREST FLOWER
("Aberfoyle, Dec. 19, 1853")

Mr Editor, - Having seen in one of your late papers "The Flower of Eramosa," and believing that there are other flowers, - for you know every lad thinks his lass the fairest - I trouble you with the following lines. If you think they are worthy of a place in your Journal, you can publish them, and you will much oblige, a lover of the girls: -

> The flower of Eramosa may
> Be fair as fair can be,
> But the bonnie flow'r o' Puslinch
> Is fairer far than she.
>
> The bard may love his lassie weel,
> And think she is divine,
> But the bonnie flow'r o' Puslinch
> More beautiful doth shine.
>
> Tho' she may be the fairest flower
> In Eramosa grows -
> Tho' she may like the lily shine,
> O'er Albion's blooming rose;
>
> Her beauty fades beneath the light
> Of this bewitching dove, -
> Her heart's the lon[..][340] of purity,
> Her voice the notes of love;

---

[339] Latin = "See and Believe."

[340] Unfortunately the original microfilm imaging makes this one word very difficult to decipher.

Her eyes they like the diamonds shine,
Her smile the dawning morn,
Her mind's the mirror of all truth -
A rose without a thorn;

Her form is cast in nature's mould,
Most beautiful to see;
Yes, Eramosa cannot boast
A maiden fair as she.

And had I but the gift of Burns
To sing my lassie's praise,
I'd crown the bonnie Puslinch flow'r
With high poetic lays. -

I'd sing her worth in love's sweet strain,
I'd let the poet know,
Guelph, Puslinch maids, and Waterloo,
Are something more than show. -

I sing the praise of one sweet flow'r,
Transparent in the dew;
In Guelph, Puslinch, are hundreds more,
The same in Waterloo.

For every laddie thinks his lass
Is worth her weight in gold;
The bard of Eramosa, then,
He should not be so bold.

But oh, I wish the mossy flow'r
The bard's fond heart may cheer,
That they may be in wedlock join'd
"Before another year."

\*\*\*

# 𝔄ppendix 𝔥

## List of Guelph Versifiers

### of the

### 19th Century

#### Chronologically according to their dates of Versifying[341]

---

1 **John Galt** 1779-1839     (section I)
2 **Samuel Strickland** 1804-1867     (section II)
3 **John Taylor** Flourished 1836     (section III)
4 **Thomas Murphy** Flourished 1846     (section IV)
5 **James McGrogan** Flourished 1847     (section V)
6 **George Pirie** 1799-1870     (section VI)
7 **John Smith** 1818-1899     (section VII)
8 **"Fanny"** Flourished 1847     (section VIII)
9 **J.H.**[342] Flourished 1848
10 **Ben Brace**[343] Flourished 1849
11 **Ben Brace (Junior)**[344] Flourished 1849
12 **"Jonathan"** Flourished 1849     (section IX)
13 **"Brother Bogie"**[345] Flourished 1849
14 **"Philo"**[346] Flourished 1850

---

[341] This list does not include all anonymous versifiers.

[342] "J.H." wrote an original poem for the *Guelph & Galt Advertiser* (printed 28 January, 1848), entitled "To Mary Eliza In Heaven." J.H. may possibly be Joseph H. Hacking, future (1873) proprietor and editor of the *Advertiser*, and proprietor of the Hacking Excelsior Printing House (1874) (see Appendix C). Certainty of J.H.'s identity must, however, be left to future research.

[343] Ben Brace wrote, from Guelph, several verses in 1849 for the *Guelph & Galt Advertiser* (see section VIII on "Jonathan"). His work was predominantly political, including "Stanzas" (6 September, 1849); "Rhymes For The Times, No. 5," which begins: "Ho, Montreal members of the League, ye lovers of mob law,..." (13 September, 1849).

[344] Ben Brace (Junior), presumably the son of Ben Brace, wrote "Rhymes For The Times, No. 1,"[53] and "An Old Yarn In New Colours" for the *Guelph & Galt Advertiser*, 16 August, 1849.

[345] "Brother Bogie" wrote an original poem for the *Guelph & Galt Advertiser* (printed 30 August, 1849), entitled "A Reminiscence Of The Midland District."

[346] The identity of the versifier using the pseudonym "Philo" remains unknown. This versifier's poem "Find Out Pride" was penned in Eramosa Township for the Guelph *Herald* in 1850, and printed in that paper 13 August, 1850.

15 **R.B.** Flourished 1853 (section X)
16 **JOHN PEARSON** Flourished 1853-1854 (section XI)
17 **J. FUDGER**[347] Flourished 1856
18 **CHARLES T. DANIEL** Flourished 1864 (section XII)
19 **J.E.C.**[348] Flourished 1866
20 **ALEXANDER MCLACHLAN**[349] Flourished 1866
21 **HETTY HAZELWOOD** Flourished 1867-1871 (section XIII)
22 **DAVID MORRISON** Flourished 1869 (section XIV)
23 **C. (THORNTON)**[350] Flourished 1869 (Appendix B)
24 **T.J. STARRET**[351] Flourished 1869-c.1876
25 **COL. WILLIAM KINGSMILL** (1794-1876)
26 **ALEXANDER W. BLYTH** Flourished 1870 (section XV)
27 **J.P.B.** Flourished 1870 (section XVI)
28 **JOHN INGLIS** 1839-1928 (section XVII)
29 **ROBERT BOYD** 1797-1880 (section XVIII)
30 **"DIOGENES REDIVIVUS"** Flourished 1875 (section XIX)
31 **A.E.L. TRELEAVEN** Flourished 1877 (section XX)
32 **CHARLES C. FOSTER** Flourished 1879 (section XXI)
33 **"MADGE"** Flourished 1879 (section XXII)
34 **J.F.M.** Flourished 1881 (section XXIII)
35 **MARGARET BEATRICE BURGESS (NÉE ANDERSON)** 1841-1900 (section XXIV)
36 **ANONYMOUS GUELPH TOURISTS** 1884 (section XXV)
37 **THOMAS LAIDLAW** 1825-1902 (section XXVI)
38 **JAMES GAY** 1810-1891 (section XXVII)
39 **GEORGE NORRISH** 1831-1912 (section XXVIII)
40 **"RICARDO"** Flourished 1887-1892 (section XXIX)
41 **JAMES MCINTYRE** 1828-1906 (section XXX)
42 **D.F.F.** Flourished 1892 (section XXXI)
43 **LT. COL. JOHN MCCRAE MD** 1872-1918 (section XXXII)

AND

44 **MALCOLM MACCORMACK** (before 1900)

\*\*\*

---

[347] J. Fudger's poem "A Dream" was written in Guelph, July of 1856 and printed in the *Weekly Advertiser* on 10 July, 1856.

[348] The identity of "J.E.C." remains unknown; they write "The Rose" for the Guelph *Herald*; printed 1 May, 1866.

[349] "Alex M'Lachlan" wrote "To A Ruined Temple" for the Guelph *Herald*; printed 28 August, 1866.

[350] See Appendix B - Thornton's Bookstore. "C." may be C[harles] Thornton, proprietor of Thornton's.

[351] Starret wrote a poem "for the Mercury" entitled "The Last Meeting," on 31 March, 1869, printed on 17 April, 1869. Douglass (c.1963) notes that "On Seeing An Indian Mother Conveying A Child's Coffin Down The Streets Of Guelph," was written by T.S. at Guelph in 1876. This poem is also ascribed to Thomas Laidlaw (section XXVI).

## FURTHER READING

Calvert, Fanny Colwill 1981. *The Diary of Fanny Colwill Calvert: Portrait of an Artist 1848-1936*. Marian Frye Colwill-Maddock (privately published).

Clark, Dr. Daniel 1900. *Selections from Scottish Canadian Poets*. Toronto: The Caledonian Society of Toronto.

Colombo, J. R. and Singer, P. (eds) 1996. *Master of all Poets; The Life and Works of James Gay, of the Royal City of Guelph, Ontario, Poet Laureate of Canada and Master of All Poets*. Toronto: Colombo & Company.

Coulman, D. E. 1977. *Guelph; Take a Look at Us!* The Boston Mills Press.

Crowley, T. 1987. The Mickle Family and Pioneering in the Guelph Area in the 1830's. In, Ruth and Eber Pollard (eds) *Historic Guelph; The Royal City*, Volume XXVI (1986-1987). Guelph: Guelph Historical Society. Pp. 4-27.

Deacon, William Arthur 1927. *The Four Jameses*. Ottawa: Graphic Publishers.

Durtnell, D.M. 1987. The History of the Macdonald-Love Block. In, Ruth and Eber Pollard (eds) *Historic Guelph; The Royal City*, Volume XXVI (1986-1987). Guelph: Guelph Historical Society. Pp. 34-47.

Edwards, David Herschell 1881. *One Hundred Modern Scottish Poets: With Biographical and Critical Notices*. Brechin: D.H. Edwards.

Golick, Greta Petronella 2010. *Frank Nunan and the Guelph Bookbindery: A Documentary Investigation* (PhD Thesis). Toronto: University of Toronto.

Hinds, A. Leone 1967. *Guelph's Brave, Squaw and Papoose*. Guelph Historical Society Publications; Volume VII, Number 8. Guelph: Guelph Historical Society.

Irwin, Ross W. 1998. *Guelph: Origin of Street Names*. Guelph: Guelph Historical Society.

Johnson, Leo A. 1977. *History of Guelph 1827-1927*. Guelph: Guelph Historical Society.

Murray, Robert 1897. *Hawick songs and song writers.*
    W. & J. Kennedy.

Prescott, J.F. 1985. *In Flanders fields: the story of John McCrae.*
    Erin, Ontario: Boston Mills Press.

Sadek, N. 1987. The Mickle Family Papers. In, Ruth and Eber Pollard (eds) *Historic Guelph; The Royal City*, Volume **XXVI** (1986-1987).
    Guelph: Guelph Historical Society. Pp. 28-33.

Stead, Hilary 2002. *Guelph; A People's Heritage 1827-2002.*
    Guelph: City of Guelph. Online pdf document at www.electricscotland.com

Stinton, James 1908. *Bibliography of Works Relating to, or Published in, Hawick.*
    Hawick: Vair & McNairn, "News" Office.

Thompson, Robert 1877. *A Brief Sketch of the Early History of Guelph.*
    Guelph: Mercury Steam Printing.

White, Robert W. (ed.) 1995. *The Poems of Robert Boyd 1797-1880.*[352]

Wiljer, C. 1990. The Poetry of Guelph. In, Ruth and Eber Pollard (eds) *Historic Guelph, The Royal City*; Volume **XXIX** 1989-1990.
    Guelph: Guelph Historical Society. Pp. 56-70.

\* \* \* \* \*
\* \* \*

---

[352] In the rare books archive of the Guelph Public Library (Main Branch).

# General Index

\*\*\*

# INDEX OF FULL POEMS (TITLE AND FIRST LINE)

## IN THE ORDER OF THEIR APPEARANCE IN THIS COLLECTION

179

\*\*\*

DAVID J. KNIGHT
NEAR MONKEY'S BRIDGE, SPEED RIVER, GUELPH - MAY, 2014
PHOTOGRAPH BY MATTHEW AZEVEDO -
PHOTOGRAPHY AND GRAPHIC EDITOR AT
*The Ontarion* NEWSPAPER (UNIVERSITY OF GUELPH)

DAVID J. KNIGHT (BA, MA, MPHIL) was born in Guelph, Ontario, Canada. He is an alumnus of Guelph and Southampton (UK). Knight has been an internationally published author since 2004, with books and articles spanning Historical Biography, Archaeology, Archaeoacoustics and Musicology. He has been celebrated by the University of Guelph as a Campus Author for his first book, *King Lucius of Britan* (2008: The History Press). He was an editorial board member of the inaugural academic Humanities journal *Hummingbird* (2010: University of Southampton, UK). Knight resides once again in Guelph, and has researched and written articles for *My Guelph* (2013), and published two books *Sound Guelph* and a new edition of John Galt's Gothic novel *The Omen*, both with Publication Studio Guelph (2013). Knight is presently the General Editor of Vocamus Editions, and begins this role with his *Guelph Versifiers of the 19th Century* (2014), a fresh thorough collection of interest to all readers and writers.

www.ingramcontent.com/pod-product-compliance
Lightning Source LLC
Chambersburg PA
CBHW031840090426
42741CB00005B/304